THE PAGEANT OF VENICE

# A BOOK OF BRIDGES

Pictures by FRANK BRANGWYN, R.A.

Text by W. SHAW SPARROW. Containing 36 Colour Plates and 36 Line Drawings. *Crown 4to.*

Also LARGE PAPER EDITION, limited to 75 Copies, for sale in England and America. Printed on hand-made paper, with an original Lithograph by FRANK BRANGWYN, R.A. *Crown Folio* (15 × 10). (*Out of print.*)

# PRINTS AND DRAWINGS BY FRANK BRANGWYN

WITH SOME OTHER PHASES OF HIS ART

By W. SHAW SPARROW. Profusely illustrated in Colour and Black and White by FRANK BRANGWYN, R.A. *Demy 4to.*

Also a SPECIAL EDITION limited to 60 numbered copies, printed on hand-made paper, containing a special Lithograph and a special Etching. (*Out of print.*)

## THE BODLEY HEAD

"THE DOGANA"

# THE PAGEANT OF VENICE

BY EDWARD HUTTON
ILLUSTRATED WITH PICTURES
AND DRAWINGS BY

## FRANK BRANGWYN, R.A.

LONDON: JOHN LANE THE BODLEY HEAD LIMITED
NEW YORK: JOHN LANE COMPANY        MCMXXII

THE MAYFLOWER PRESS, PLYMOUTH, ENGLAND.    WILLIAM BRENDON AND SON, LTD.

TO

## SIR WALTER BECKER, K.B.E.

WHO BY PERSONAL SERVICE, SELF-SACRIFICE AND GENEROSITY

DURING A LONG LIFE IN ITALY:

BY HIS NOBLE SUPPORT IN WAR OF

## THE BRITISH RED CROSS IN ITALY:

AND IN PEACE OF

## THE BRITISH INSTITUTE OF FLORENCE

HAS HELPED WITH ALL HIS MIGHT

TO FOSTER THE ANCIENT FRIENDSHIP BETWEEN

## ITALY AND ENGLAND

# CONTENTS

# LIST OF PLATES

# THE PAGEANT OF VENICE

# THE PAGEANT OF VENICE

## I

## THE BEGINNINGS.

EVERYONE who has come into Venice from the mainland of Italy, whether by boat from Fusina or Chioggia, or by the railway bridge from Mestre over the lagoon, must have wondered, seeing the glory of the city rise before him out of the sea, how such a place came to be founded, and who were the first to establish themselves thus in the midst of the waters, and why they left the security of *terra firma* for the mud-banks and islands of the salt lagoon.

It is in Torcello, perhaps, that that question is best answered, for it was in Torcello that Venice was born. It is true there is next to nothing to see in Torcello—an old and broken church, a ruin and a crazy tower ; but if you need more to tell you the secret of the place, there are the waterways that sing and sob, night and day, calling you, calling you to come and discover a ruined kingdom, a secret island, and a whole world of forgotten things, that the marsh and the lagoon guard and keep from the destroying hands of men. And there, if you stay

B

1

long enough, in the evening shadow, when the tourists have all gone back to Venice on their steamer, when the children have finished their evening play, when the mothers are all busy with gossip, and the good-men are half asleep in their doorways, Torcello will tell you her story, and you will understand why the water is always calling you to come away, why there is so much silence, why the tower is so crazy, and one church broken and the other a ruin.

For Torcello was built in haste, in the midst of flight, founded upon fear. When the tall towers of Altinum were burned, when the city went up in flames and no man thought of standing any more, but all men were in full flight for the marsh and the sea, they came to this island and hastily built what they could; and in memory of their burned home called the place Torcello, and from Torcello is Venice sprung. You may see it all from that crazy tower, where the door swings on its hinges in the evening wind, and no man passes by—Altinum, Torcello, Venice, they all lie at your feet. Those who came so long ago, and built the place, had known what it was to be utterly dispossessed, to be broken, to be beggared, to be dishonoured, and by barbarians. At last they had wondered where they should look for a hiding-place, and when by a sort of miracle they came to Torcello they rested, and built in haste—always in haste—hardly, and with what material they could bring from their ruins, a church and a tower that should serve them and remind them a little of their home. Such, doubt-less, was the origin of S. Fosca and the cathedral of S. Maria; such, doubtless, was the beginning of that crazy tower.

The pageant of Venice really began thus at the beginning, when, as the unknown author of the Chronicle of Altinum tells us, directed

2

by signs from Heaven, and under the protection of the Saints, the people of Altinum, led by their Bishop, fled in their boats and sought refuge from the barbarians on the islands of the lagoon. But the flight of which he speaks was in fact not the first, rather it was the last. It is possible that the first was caused by the fall of Aquileia before Attila in the year 452. But from that flight there was a return. It was not till the time of the Lombard invasion that the final exodus took place, and Torcello was built (568). It is of this that the chronicler speaks, and the story he tells, though it has received a certain atmosphere of superstition from the Dark Age, may be accepted without much question.

It is certain that when the Roman administration began to fail, in every Roman city there had appeared a personage who was perhaps better acquainted with its life than anyone else; who had more power than anyone else over its thought and its moral and who in very many cases really administered its affairs; that personage was the Bishop. It is therefore not extraordinary to learn from the Chronicle that it was the Bishop Paulus of Altinum who led the final exodus from that city to the lagoons, nor that he should be named as the founder of the encampment, which was to become the City and State of Venice.

The story of the flight is picturesque enough in its simplicity. In the time of Bishop Paul, says the chronicler,[1] there came from the West a pestilence of cruel pagans; they destroyed the cities as they came, but the multitude of divers people who had sought safety in Altinum, together with its own citizens, were preserved by a sign from God. For suddenly all the birds which dwelt in the many towers which surrounded the

[1] Cronaca Altinate in *Arch. Stor. Ital.*, I, viii, p. 54.

3

city took flight, carrying their little ones in their beaks, and all the people, when they were shewn this sign, made ready to depart also, and many, indeed, fled at once to Ravenna and to Istria and the Pentapolis. But those that were left fasted three days, so that God should shew them whither they should go, whether by road or sea, that they might live. And presently a voice was heard, like a trumpet, which said to them : " Go up into the tower and look upon the stars." And the Bishop went up, and looking forth he saw the stars, which appeared like islands in the lagoon ; and he led his people forth, in their boats and skiffs, and they came in safety to the islands, and were saved.

Now, as the chronicler tells, there were with Paulus the Bishop, a priest, possibly his chaplain, named Maurus, another priest named Geminianus, and two knights, Arius and Avator. To Maurus it was given to see in a vision : " As I went along the *lido* a great cloud all of white, and within, as it were, two stars like the sun for brightness, and I heard a voice like unto many waters, saying : ' I am the Saviour and Lord of all the earth ; that ground whereon thou art I give to thee, build there a church in My name ' ; and after I heard another voice, softer than the morning dew, which said : ' I am Mary, Mother of Our Lord Jesus Christ, I would that thou build a church in my honour also.' " Nor were these all the visions he had, for S. Peter, Prince of the Apostles, S. Autolinus, S. Giustina, and S. John Baptist also appeared to him. What are we to make of all this ?

Perhaps the interpretation may lie in the fact that the flight of 568 was not the first, and that the people of Altinum not only found the aboriginal fishermen upon the islands and already in possession, but the old fugitives also ; and that, well armed as they would have been,

4

"RIO DI S. TROVASO"

the newcomers, headed by the two knights, needed some heavenly sanction for their probably forcible seizure of the islands. Hence these visions. It may be so. Thus Christ and the Blessed Virgin and the Saints give the land to the people. They were thus the only suzeraines. You do not admit an earthly sovereign if you can obtain an heavenly. Venice never did. " God who is our help and protector has saved us that we might dwell upon these waters. This second Venetia which we have raised in the lagoons is a mighty habitation for us. No power of Emperor or Prince can reach us, and of them we have no fear." It was in these words that the State of Venice was founded—the first nation, a Latin nation too, to emerge out of the ruins of the Empire. In the quarrel of East and West that claim ever grew clearer, yet it must not be forgotten that Venice, thus founded on the sea, looked, in fact, East, and though never pledging herself, did for her own ends make a formal act of submission to Byzantium, and that Maurice the Cappadocian in 584 conferred her first diploma upon her as a separate State.

Venice looked East, too, in an economic as well as a political sense. Was it for this that she chose S. Theodore as her first patron, S. Theodore who had been martyred for breaking an idol, such as the crocodile on which he stands in the Piazza—the Dragon of old Egypt?

S. Theodore was the patron of the older Venetian State. When the inevitable quarrels between the islands and the island families had been disposed of, when the Dogeship had finally been settled as non-hereditary, and an oligarchical State founded to embrace all the islands and *lidi*, she chose another patron and protector. Perhaps her thoughts turned back to the past, and she remembered her origin. At any rate,

5

she put herself under the protection of him who founded the Church of Aquileia, who was reported to have been cast upon the Venetian shore, and had there in his distress heard the voice of the Lord saying : "Pax tibi, Marce, Evangelista meus." If the flight from Altinum and the advent to the islands was the first pageant of Venice, the second was surely the coming of S. Mark.

S. Peter had sent S. Mark into Egypt, and he had ended his life there, martyred by the infidels as Bishop of Alexandria, then the second city of the world. Venice not only remembered her origin, but, as I have said, she looked East. Her devotion to S. Mark was probably increased by the fact that the body of the Evangelist lay in Alexandria in the power of the Mussulman, with whom the Venetians had been obliged by the Emperor Leo to forego all intercourse, even for purposes of trade. Venice looked East, and it may be that that prohibition of trade with the infidel was largely the cause of what followed.

At any rate, two Venetian merchants, called in the chronicles Buono da Malamocco and Rustico da Torcello, in 839 found themselves in Alexandria, where the Christians were in great misery by reason of the looting of their churches by the Mussulmans for the adornment of the mosques and palaces ; and it was rumoured that the Sultan was about to destroy the church in which the body of S. Mark lay, in order to use the materials elsewhere for his own purposes. They made up their minds what to do, and with much difficulty, and the help of the monk Staurizius and the priest Theodore, they managed to steal the body of the Saint, and, putting it in a cart and covering it with salt pork, which the Mussulmans held as unclean, they passed through the port and came to their ship and put to sea. After a tremendous voyage, in which

6

they near lost their ship, they arrived in the lagoons, and, their news having reached Venice already, were met by the whole city in procession, headed by the Doge and the clergy, who brought the body in procession to the shore, and the nobles of Venice bore the precious treasure on their shoulders from the ship to the chapel of the Doge's Palace, to the church of S. Teodoro, that is, where it was to remain until a special church could be built for it. Buono and Rustico were pardoned, and from that moment S. Mark became the patron of the Republic instead of S. Theodore.

What can Venice have been like when she became in the middle of the ninth century the city of S. Mark? Unhappily we have no means of knowing; but we may perhaps gather an impression by chance from the chronicles.

Cassiodorus, the friend and secretary of Theodoric the Great, who at the end of the disastrous fifth century secured for Italy a peace of more than thirty years, has left us a description of the first Venetian settlement which brings it visibly before our eyes. He shews us a people largely engaged in fishery, and for the most part living on what they could win from the sea. They had driven piles into the mud to hold the land from the tide, binding these piles together with wattles and rushes. They had conserved the rainfall in *pozzi*, and their dwellings were all made of wattle, "built like sea-birds' nests, half on sea and half on land, spread, as the Cyclades, over the surface of the waters."

But it cannot have been for long that Venice remained a mere settlement. At any rate, with the flight of 568, with the destruction of Altinum, and the realization of the hopelessness of any return, the fugitives must have been able to bring materials, brick and stone, from

7

the ruins on the mainland, so that what was at first a refuge must soon have become a home, and at last the city of Venice. Such brick houses as were set up may probably still be seen almost anywhere on the islands of the lagoon, though not in Venice itself. They were one story high, built about a courtyard, where the corn would be beaten out in June and July, and the fish dried. Above the house ran an open loggia, whence one might see and signal to those far out on the vague waters. Before the house, between it and the lagoon, a path or roadway was built of beaten mud, strengthened with piles and guarded with wattles ; this was called, as it still is, *fundamenta*, and was a continuation of the actual foundation of the house. But no doubt most of the houses were still light constructions of wood, which did not bear too heavily on the insecure mud-banks. In the better houses there was a fire-place, with a chimney, and this seems to have been a peculiarity of Venice. And there were trees.

But whatever the city may have looked like in the middle of the Dark Ages, whether it was more largely of brick than we believe, or thatched or tiled, it lacked every characteristic feature of the city of to-day, except the waterways. There was no Campanile, though the piles were already being driven to carry it ; the church of S. Theodore was in the form of a great cross, but it seems to have been covered with thatch. The Doge's Palace, though it was no doubt the most important and substantial house in Venice, was nothing like what we see, and there were no bridges.

No doubt the greater buildings of the city were the churches, which were built in basilical form, and contained all that had been secured or brought away from the mainland cities.

8

But though such a Venice was very different from the city we have known, the centres of its life were the same, the Piazza and the Rialto, and though we should not recognize them, perhaps, could we see them —the Piazza was divided in its length by a canal called the Rivo Battario —we may think of them as what they were, coeval with Venice and the cradle of the life of the Venetian State, where the Venetians, then dressed in long, girdled tunics, covered with a mantle in winter, most did congregate, and where the most enduring of all the Italian States was conceived and born.

## II

## THE ESPOUSAL OF THE SEA.

THE greatness of Venice, like the greatness of England, was founded upon the sea and upon the wealth which the sea can give—foreign trade. It was to be built up and conserved again, as in England, by an oligarchic form of government and administration, in form aristocratic, though, as with us, birth was to count for very little, and ability for almost everything, the aristocracy refreshing itself by co-option and marriage. The aristocratic oligarchy which thus administered and controlled the Venetian State, in which no hereditary or democratic principle was recognized, was not achieved all at once—or, indeed, without a long struggle. It was not till 1023 that it was finally decided that the Dogeship could not be established as an hereditary office, and it was not till 1171 that the movement to deprive the people of their part in the government began, and not till after 1319 that it accomplished itself.

It may be that the sea, and what we call the command of the sea—an ambition Venice never set aside till it was achieved—had more than a little to do with all this. The command of the sea, at any rate, has never been attempted by a democracy, for it might seem to demand too persistent, too far-sighted, and too self-denying an effort. It was in this effort that Venice became, as England did later, an aristocratic oligarchy represented by a constitutional sovereign—in England hereditary, in Venice elective.

The nobles of Venice, those " more prominent " citizens of which we read, seem to have been very much what the nobles were in the cities of the mainland, that is to say, unruly and intent on private war. Thus the Caloprini and the Morosini, for example, involved themselves and involved Venice in their vendetta, even appealing for foreign aid, which, but for the sea, might have ruined the young State at the beginning. They were, however, crushed by Doge Pietro Orseolo II (983–1008), who may be said to have laid the foundations of the maritime supremacy of Venice. But the Orseolo were ambitious to found a dynasty as the Particiachi and the Candiani had done before them. They were perpetually excluded from office, and by the year 1032 the aristocracy was ready to take control. In that year two councillors were appointed to assist the Doge, and it is in the work thus begun we see the beginning of the establishment of the true oligarchy. It was determined to make the Doge a figure-head, a mere constitutional sovereign, and to take all political power out of the hands of the people. These two achievements were, in fact, complementary, for the people had been used to elect the Doge. The ceremony took place in S. Pietro di Castello, the Cathedral of Venice, the Bishop and clergy assisting. After the election the Doge was carried back on the barge of State, later the Bucintoro, to S. Mark's, which he entered barefooted, as a sign of

11

humility. It was from the high altar there he took his staff of office and proceeded to the Ducal Palace, amid the shouts of the people. There he took the oath, and began to re-order the place spoiled by the mob.

This election seems to have been the right of the people till 1192, when, enormously enriched by the business of the Crusades, "the most prominent citizens," justified by the folly of the populace, which had urged Doge Vitale Michiel II to the miserable campaign of 1171, to avenge their compatriots in Constantinople, whom the Emperor Manuel had seized, murdered the Doge and established a new form of election in which the people had no part. They established the Greater Council, formed by two representatives from each of the Sestieri, the divisions, of the city. The business was to elect the Doge, " if the people pleased," to appoint all officers of the State, and to choose the members of the General Assembly. This General Assembly consisted of 480 members, each member of the Greater Council appointing forty to serve for one year. The Greater Council also now appointed six officers instead of two to advise the Doge. From this time the reality of the Dogeship becomes less and less, and by the end of the thirteenth century the oligarchy was finally established, when in 1297 it was decided that all those who had sat on the Greater Council during the last five years should " ballot one by one, and that those only who received twelve votes should be members of the Greater Council," and further, that only those should be eligible who could prove that their ancestors had sat in the Council between the years 1172 and 1297. It was further enacted that these provisions could not be repealed except with the consent of five out of six ducal councillors, twenty-five of the

12

"THE GRAND CANAL"

Council of forty, and two-thirds of the Greater Council itself. This measure was known as the closing of the Greater Council. In 1319 the Libro d'Oro, or full register of the political aristocracy, thus established in power, was opened, and during the first half of the fourteenth century all this new administration was firmly established and set in order, and we see clearly appear the Senate of one hundred and twenty to manage foreign affairs, finance, customs, and naval defence. The six councillors of the Doge already alluded to become the Lesser Council, and a new Council of Forty is appointed to act as the judicial authority of the State. In fact, by 1335 we have really complete the constitution of Venice, which was to uphold that great State for very many centuries. It can only be compared for strength and endurance to the English oligarchy from 1668 to 1832.

Thus Venice established herself. Really independent of both Emperors, politically dependent neither on the East nor the West, she built up her enormous trade on the sea, and by reason of this became, as we shall see, necessary to Europe in the great adventures of the Middle Age. Nor did she fail to turn this necessity to her own advantage.

But if Venice was thus politically independent of the Imperial power, there was a government of which she had to take account. This was the Papacy, and her relations with this, the greatest of all elective monarchies, and the most enduring, are of very great interest. To begin with, we must note that though politically Venice leaned to the East, as her formal act of submission in 584 serves to shew, in philosophy and religion she was always wholly of the West. Her Patriarchate was a Western Patriarchate dependent upon Rome, and her religion was

13

that of all Western Christendom. She held the Catholic Faith. It is not surprising, therefore, that when the Emperor Barbarossa, in the twelfth century, quarrelled with the Pope, Alexander III, and immediately in the confusion which followed proclaimed a Pope of his own —an antipope, Victor IV—Venice sided with Alexander III. That this action also served to solve the quarrel of the Venetian Bishop of Grado with the Archbishop of Aquileia, and indirectly, nearly three hundred years later, to lead to the creation of the Patriarchate of Venice, goes for little. Venice forced the rebellious Archbishop of Aquileia to submit to Pope Alexander. He was a fugitive in France, and the Italian bishops who stood to his cause found a refuge in Venice. There followed the Lombard League and the defeat of Barbarossa and Legnano. The Pope, a wanderer on the face of the earth, was then in Anagni, when it was arranged that a meeting should take place between Pope and Emperor at some city in Northern Italy. Venice was chosen.

An amazing legend has grown up around this famous meeting. It is said that Alexander III came to Venice disguised as a pilgrim, and, still a fugitive, unknown and unrecognized, having nowhere to lay his head, he spent the night in the porch of the church of S. Salvatore, in the Sestiere of S. Marco. A second night he spent wandering for hours through the dark, narrow, winding ways of the city, till at dawn he knocked at the door of a building he took to be a convent, which was, indeed, S. Maria della Carità. Admitted, he was employed in the kitchen as a scullion for no less than six months, till he was recognized by a French monk who had often seen him in France, and who at once informed the Doge. The amazing, the tremendous news, spread through the city. The people were seized with frenzied emotion ; the Ducal

14

Palace and the whole city and port were overwhelmed with excitement.
A vast procession was formed and proceeded under banners, with the
Patriarch of Grado, the clergy, the Doge, and all the officers of the
State to bring the Vice-gerent of God from the monastic kitchen to the
Palace of the Patriarch.

Thence the Pope sent ambassadors to Barbarossa. The Emperor
replied with a threat of war against the Republic. Sixty galleys from
Genoa and Pisa appeared in the Adriatic under the command of the
Emperor's son. Against this great fleet Venice could only muster thirty
ships. But the Doge knelt before the Pope, who blessed him and
promised him victory. On Ascension Day the two fleets met off Salvore,
and the Venetians were victorious. Forty-eight enemy galleys were
taken and a vast number of prisoners, including the Emperor's son, who
was at once sent back to his father. Moved by the generosity of the
Pope, the Emperor asked for permission to come to Venice. He came,
but found it a Canossa. At last, having laid aside his crown and sceptre
and all his royal robes, he was admitted to the Pope's presence in the
central porch of S. Mark's. There he laid him down flat upon his
face while the Pope placed his foot upon his neck. The Emperor made
a last effort, saying : " Not to you do I kneel, but to Peter." But the
Pope answered : " Both to me and to Peter."

All this you may see painted in the halls of the Doge's Palace. There
seems, however, to be little if any truth in the whole story. Its value
for us lies in this : that the legend bears witness to a fact, namely, the
victory of the Pope, and largely by means of Venice, over the Emperor ;
and in this, too, that it was on account of this victory that Venice
obtained from the Pope the titular dominion of the sea, which title

15

was renewed every Ascension Day in the great ceremony of the Espousal of the Adriatic.

The claim of Venice to the command of the Adriatic was inherent in her position both geographical and economic ; and it seems to have become conscious, at any rate, as early as the year 997. As her trade came into existence it became every year more necessary to her to secure the absolute safety of her commerce, of which the pirates of the Dalmatian coasts made a prey.

It was Doge Pietro Orseolo II who fitted out the first great expedition against these pirates, and the fleet sailed on Ascension Day, 997. It was altogether successful, and every year thereafter the victory was celebrated by the Republic on this day in a dramatic ceremony, as though to impress upon her people their dependence upon, and in consequence the necessity of, their mastery of the sea. From that day in 997 it had been the custom of the Doge, on the anniversary of the departure of the fleet—that is, on Ascension Day—to go forth from the Porto di Lido in his State barge, accompanied by the Bishop and the Council and the principal members of the State, followed by almost the whole city, and there upon the sea to perform certain ceremonies. This great festa had been celebrated for one hundred and eighty years when Pope Alexander III came to Venice, and received at once the hospitality and the political assistance of the Republic. His gratitude was shewn in a very remarkable investiture which he conferred upon the city. Venice demanded and obtained from the Pope the Investiture of the Adriatic. He conferred upon the city the Lordship of that sea, and he gave to the Doge a ring with which he was to wed the Adriatic, for he desired that this ceremony of marriage should be added to the old

16

ceremony that took place outside the Porto di Lido, and on Ascension Day. Therefore when the Doge's barge arrived outside the port the poop was presented to the sea, and the Bishop, blessing the ring, presented it to the Doge before he poured out the Holy Water from a vase upon the waters wherein the Doge must throw the ring, saying these words : *Mare, ti sposiamo in segno del nostro vero e perpetuo dominio*. O Sea, we wed thee in sign of our true and perpetual dominion.

Thus was shewn to all the people that the relations between Venice and the sea were not less close than those between a man and his wife —that Venice and the sea were one.

To this festa, which was known as the Festa della Sensa, that is, of the Ascension, enormous crowds of strangers came, for it was the season of pilgrimages, and the time of its final establishment was the era of the Crusades. The spectacle took on the form of a triumph, after the fall of Constantinople, and all Europe heard of its splendour and fame. As the Doge went forth to wed the sea, he was accompanied not only by the Signoria, the Senate, and nearly all the Great Council, but by the ambassadors of the Courts of Europe, who assisted at the function, sat beside His Serenity, and would appear in some sort to have sanctioned this act of possession, and to have confirmed the rights of the Republic.

It was at this time, it would seem, that the Doge's barge received the name of the *Bucintoro*, perhaps a corruption from the word Ducentorum, because it was manned by two hundred men. However this may be, it was a vessel specially constructed for this ceremony, and perfectly adapted to it ; a floating palace divided into two *piani* or

D

17

stages, 100 feet long by 21 broad. On the first stage were the rowers; the upper stage, covered with crimson velvet and ornamented with cloth of gold, embroideries and gold lace, formed a *salone* of the whole length of the vessel, heightened towards the poop, where a little window opened, through which the Doge threw the ring into the sea. This window was placed behind the gorgeous *sedia* of the Doge, which stood on a platform two steps above the rest of the *salone*. The poop itself consisted of a naval victory with trophies. Above, two *putti* held a shell, which formed the Ducal *baldacchino*. On either side of the *sedia* stood a statue of Prudence and Energy (Forza). On either side of these, but lower than the *sedia*, were seats covered with rich stuffs, for the Patriarch, the Ambassadors, the Signoria, and the Governors of the arsenal. The tribune was also ornamented with bas-reliefs, gilded, of Apollo and the Muses, and these were continued round the *salone*, in representation of the art of shipbuilding and so forth. The whole floor of the *salone* was occupied with the suite of the Doge, and such distinguished strangers as might be invited to make part of it. Such was the vessel of the Doge, as it passed with its 168 rowers over the lagoon to Porto di Lido, bearing on its prow a colossal statue of Justice. These rowers were neither gondoliers nor sailors, but the *Arsenalotti*, the craftsmen of the arsenal, who composed the most beloved guild of the Republic. It was their privilege to conduct the Doge to this marriage with the sea.

Certain great gilded barges followed the *Bucintoro* conveying the clergy and the suites of the ambassadors. These were followed by a great number of galleys, and these by every sort of boat belonging to the *uffiziali di mare*.

18

The Doges *de' Nicolotti*, that is, those who inhabited the contrada di S. Niccolò, had also a particular barge, for they came of the island of fishermen. The glove-makers also had a place and certain privileges on this day. But, as may well be imagined, the real animation of the festa came from the innumerable crowd of boats which followed the official procession, and quite covered the lagoon from the Piazzetta to the Lido, with music and singing : the nobles, the merchants, the guilds of various sorts, each and all had their various boats all festooned with laurels and with flowers. The innumerable bells rang out, and, as the centuries went by, the cannon from the arsenal and the islands added their voices to the enormous clamour of the greatest and the noblest of Venetian festivals.

## III

## THE FOURTH CRUSADE.

THAT Venice was in fact mistress of the sea, that this glorious ceremony was not a mere boast, but represented a reality, is attested by the most amazing event of the thirteenth century—the Fall of Constantinople before the Crusaders, led by Venice, in 1204. Happily we have the account of an eye-witness, not a Venetian, who has left us a record of this tremendous adventure, every line of which bears witness to the great position of Venice.

The Fourth Crusade was preached, as we know, by Fulk of Neuilly, priest and curate of Neuilly, a village between Lagny sur Marne and Paris, and launched by Pope Innocent III. The Barons of France and Flanders held a parliament at Soissons in 1200 to determine when they should depart, and what way it would be most prudent to take; but they could determine nothing, because it appeared to them that the number of the crusaders was then insufficient. Two months later they assembled again at Compiegne, however, and appointed ambassadors to arrange all things necessary for the great undertaking. The ambassadors chosen were six, and to these six the Barons confided the whole negotiations, furnishing them with letters patent, whereby they engaged to make good all the engagements which these six should enter into on their behalf, at the ports and other places. The six envoys departed, and consulting together they were of opinion that they should find a greater number of ships at Venice than at any other port, and hastening thither with all diligence they arrived in that city in the first week in Lent.

It is Villehardouin, one of the ambassadors, who gives us an account of what followed:

"Enrico Dandolo was then Doge, a man of extraordinary worth and capacity. He received the ambassadors with much distinction, and both he and all Venice were much pleased at their arrival. But when they delivered the letters of their lords, the Venetians marvelled greatly what could be the object which brought them to Venice. For the letters were letters of credence by which the barons desired them to credit the bearers as themselves, for that they would make good all that their envoys should undertake on their behalf. To this the Doge replied: 'My lords, I have read your letters, and know that with the exception of crowned kings, the princes who have sent you are the most powerful in Christendom; they desire me to give credence to your words, and to hold as truth whatever you may engage; tell us, therefore, what it is you desire.' The envoys answered: 'Sir, if it please you to assemble your council, in their presence we will declare the wishes of our lords, even to-morrow if you approve of it.' The Doge answered that he desired grace until the fourth day, and then he would assemble his council, and they might make known their demands.

"They waited until the fourth day as the Doge had appointed, and

21

then repaired to the palace, which was wonderfully splendid and magnificent, and, having found the Doge and his council in the hall, they delivered their messages in these terms : ' Sir, we are come to thee from the most potent barons of France, who have put on the sign of the Cross, to avenge the wrongs of Jesus Christ, and to recover Jerusalem, if such be the will of God ; and because they know that no nation has the power of you and your people, they implore you in God's name to look with pity upon the Holy Land, and by supplying them with ships and means for their passage thither to join with them in avenging the shames of our Redeemer.'

" ' On what conditions ? ' demanded the Doge.

" ' On any conditions,' replied the envoys, ' which you may think proper to impose, provided they are within our power.'

" ' Certainly,' said the Doge, ' the request is no slight one, and the enterprise itself is of vast magnitude ; we will return you our answer in eight days ; and wonder not that we ask so long a time, for a thing of this importance needs much deliberation.' "

The term fixed by the Doge having expired, the ambassadors returned to the palace. It is unnecessary to relate all that passed there, but the conclusion of the conference was as follows : " Lords," said the Doge, " we will now declare what we have resolved on, provided our Great Council and the commons of the city consent ; and do you consider whether you will assent to our proposal. We will furnish you with ships for 4500 horses and 9000 esquires, and with ships for 4500 knights and 20,000 serjeants on foot ; we will also engage to supply men and horses with provisions for nine months, on condition of receiving four marks for every horse and two marks for every man. We

22

will observe all these engagements for one year from the day of our departure from the port of Venice; to undertake the service of God and Christendom in whatever waters that service may land us. The sum to be paid us, according to these conditions, will amount to 85,000 marks, and we will moreover undertake to equip fifty galleys for the love of God, on condition that so long as our alliance shall continue all the conquests we may make by sea or by land shall be divided equally between us. Now, decide whether you will accede to our terms."

The ambassadors replied that they would consult together and give their reply on the morrow. The same night they discussed the conditions among themselves and resolved to accept them; and on the following morning they came before the Doge and said: "Sir, we are prepared to sign this covenant." The Doge said he must lay the matter before the people, and would communicate to them what the people should resolve upon. The next day, which was the third, the Doge summoned his Great Council, which was composed of forty of the wisest persons of the land, and so wrought upon them by his wit and wisdom, which were both brilliant and profound, that they consented to what he proposed. Afterwards he treated with one hundred persons, then with two hundred, then with one thousand, that they might approve and consent; and at last he assembled more than ten thousand people in the Church of S. Mark, which is the most magnificent of churches, and prayed them that first they would hear the Mass of the Holy Ghost and then implore God to inspire them to do His pleasure in respect of the demands of the ambassadors. And the people readily obeyed him.

"When the Mass was over the Doge sent to the ambassadors,

23

desiring that they would humbly move the people to decree the conclusion of the treaty. The ambassadors repaired to the church, and were eagerly regarded by those who had not yet beheld them. Geoffrey de Villehardouin, Marshal of Champagne (who relates this), spoke by consent for the rest, and said : ' Signiors, the most high and powerful barons of France have sent us to Venice to implore you to look with pity on the Holy City, which is in bondage to the Infidels, and for God's sake to join them in avenging the wrongs of Jesus Christ. They turn to you because they know none others so powerful on the seas, and they have enjoined us to kneel at your feet until you have granted their prayers and have compassion upon the land oversea.' The six ambassadors then fell on their knees with many tears, and the Doge and people waved their hands, and cried aloud with one voice : ' We consent. We consent.' The acclamations and tumult were so great that it seemed that the earth shook, and when that great and heart-moving cry, which exceeded all human experience, had subsided, the Doge mounted to the pulpit and spoke to the people. I cannot repeat all the fair sayings of the Doge, but thus was the affair accomplished, and it was arranged that on the feast of S. John in the year 1202 the barons and pilgrims should assemble at Venice, where the vessels and all things necessary should be in readiness.

"So things befell, and in the year 1202, between the feasts of Easter and Pentecost, the pilgrims began to depart from their homes, and many tears were shed upon their departure by their friends and kinsmen. They took the road of Burgundy, Mount Jura, Mount Cenis, and Lombardy, and so began to assemble at Venice, where they encamped on an island near the port called the Isle of S. Nicholas.

24

"A great number of them, and among them Baldwin, Count of Flanders, had already arrived at Venice, when intelligence came that many were journeying by other ways to take their passage from other ports. This news caused great consternation among the pilgrims, because those who were already assembled were too few to fulfil the treaty or pay the subsidy engaged to the Venetians; they therefore resolved among themselves to send envoys to the pilgrims and to Louis, Count of Blois, who had not yet arrived in Venice to exhort and implore them to have compassion upon the land oversea and to depart from no other port but Venice. Meantime the Venetians supplied them in abundance with everything requisite for their horses and their men; the fleet which they had prepared was so gallantly equipped that Christian man had never seen its equal, and the ships, the galleys, and the barges were in such numbers that they were thrice too numerous for the diminished host of the crusaders. Ha! What a curse it was that so many sought other ports and came not to join the army, for then had Christendom been exalted and the land of the Infidels subdued.

"The Venetians having well performed and even exceeded their engagements, and being fully prepared to sail, called upon the counts and barons to pay down the sum stipulated in the treaty. The money for the transport of the army being then to be levied, there were many who declared they could pay nothing, so that the barons were compelled to take what they could. And when they had paid over all they could collect, there was still a great sum deficient. Indeed after all, though you might see numbers of rich vessels of gold and silver carried to the Doge's Palace to make up the necessary payment, there were more than 34,000 marks of silver wanting, whereat those who had

E

concealed their wealth, in the determination to contribute nothing, were exceedingly elated, imagining that thereby the army would be dispersed ; but God, who confounds the crafty, ordained it otherwise.

"The Doge then assembled his countrymen, and said to them : 'Signiors, these people can pay us no more, and as they are unable to fulfil their agreement we might retain all that they have already paid ; but such a proceeding would be an act of injustice which would bring us dishonour, and we therefore propose to them this alternative. The King of Hungary has taken from us Zara, one of the strongest places in the world, nor shall we ever recover it, except by the assistance of these crusaders ; but we propose to them, therefore, to assist us therein, and we will respite the payment of the 30,000 marks of silver which they owe us until it shall please God to grant us some rich conquest.

"On Sunday the Venetians and the greater part of the barons and pilgrims joyfully assembled in the church of S. Mark, where, before the beginning of Mass, Enrico Dandolo, the Doge, ascended the pulpit and addressed the people, saying : 'Signiors, you are accounted with the bravest people in the world for the highest enterprise that mortal man hath ever undertaken. I am a very old man, feeble in health, and have more need of repose than of glory ; yet knowing none more capable of guiding and commanding you than myself, who am your lord, if it be your pleasure that I should take the sign of the Cross to watch over and direct you, and leave my son in my place to protect our country, I will cheerfully go, and live and die with you and with the pilgrims.' The Venetians on hearing this speech cried aloud with one voice : 'We beseech you, in God's name, to do as you have said and go with us.' Much pity was excited, and many tears were shed, among the people

26

of the country and the pilgrims because of this brave old man, who had so much need of repose, both on account of his great age and inasmuch as he was nearly blind, his sight having been injured by a wound in the head, and yet now of such undaunted courage. Ha! how little do they resemble him who skulked to other ports to avoid danger!

"The ships and galleons of the barons then set sail, and fitted as they were with arms and provisions, knights, and serjeants, the shields suspended along the sides and the gay banners displayed from the turrets of the vessels, by God it was a most glorious prospect. A nobler armament never sailed from port than this, in the year of Our Lord Jesus Christ 1202."

It was October. The towering great ships *Aquila*, *Pellegrino* and *Paradiso*, flying the banner of S. Mark, led the van. Zara fell.

Then a new plan was opened. Boniface, Marquis of Monferrat, is said to have been the author of it; but it suited well the will of Venice. Not Jerusalem, but Constantinople was to be the goal. And Dandolo led them on: he forced the Dardanelles and turned the Golden Horn, and took the Imperial City in 1204.

It was then that Venice found herself. How tell of the booty! Zara was hers, the coast of Dalmatia and Crete; to her fell the Cyclades and the Sporades. She held the gateways of the East, not only the Adriatic but the whole Eastern Mediterranean was in her grip. And home she brought the great bronze horses of Constantine, to set them up over the porches of S. Mark's,[1] and their bridles were broken.

That there rose directly out of the success of this wonderful adventure

[1] They were first set up in the arsenal; but it was thought they were not conspicuous enough there.

the greatest naval struggle of the Middle Age, the struggle between Venice and Genoa for the mastery of the sea, which fills some hundred and seventy years of Venetian history, cannot be denied. Yet it was a glorious undertaking, and though Christendom deplored it, it was not to be denied that the barbarous cruelty of the Byzantines to the Crusaders in the past, in a very real way justified it. It is even rumoured that Dandolo himself, the heroic old Doge, had been blinded in Constantinople.

The great struggle with Genoa began and centred in Acre: it was pursued in Constantinople itself and continued in the Black Sea; the fourth and final round was fought by Vettor Pisani, the great Venetian admiral, brought out of prison to overthrow the Genoese; which he did with Carlo Zeno at Chioggia in 1380: and Venice became sole mistress of the Mediterranean.

In the pageant of Venice that long struggle and that final victory have their part; but in Venice itself the whole of the fourteenth century might seem to be full, not of this great struggle, but of the mysterious series of Conspiracies which are connected with the names of Bocconico, Tiepolo, and Marino Faliero.

## IV

## THE CONSPIRACIES.

IT will be remembered that it was during the fourteenth century that Venice succeeded in depriving the people of any part in the government, and finally established herself as an oligarchy in which the Dogeship was merely a constitutional office without real power. The three Conspiracies which fill the century would seem, roughly, to have been attempts on the part of certain factions of the nobles to use the opportunity of the transition and of the discontent of the people to establish the Dogeship as a tyranny similar to those which obtained in the cities on the mainland, and, above all, to establish it as an hereditary office in some family.

The three great Conspiracies remain obscure. That of Bocconico broke out in the year 1300. Bocconico was a very wealthy man, a rich burgher-merchant, outside the aristocratic families who held power in Venice. His intelligence seems to have been mediocre. His plot was discovered, and he was seized with his ten accomplices, imprisoned in the dungeons of the Ducal Palace, and hanged head downwards with

29

his fellow-conspirators between the columns near the Porta della Carta.

The Tiepolo conspiracy followed in 1310. With Baiamonte Tiepolo his wife's family, the Quirini, are involved, with others, notably the Badoers. All these families were aristocratic and of the Great Council, the closing of which they opposed. This conspiracy, too, was a hopeless failure. Tiepolo and his fellows were beaten in the Piazza. Quirini was killed, Badoer executed, and Tiepolo fled. Just as the Collegio, or Cabinet of Seven, later of Six, had been called into existence by the war of Ferrara (1308); so the famous Council of Ten was called into existence by the Tiepolo conspiracy. It supplied a committee, secret and swift in action, to deal with a crisis within the State. The Council of Ten thus began, as a temporary committee of Public Safety, to carry out the will of the oligarchy; it remained as a permanent institution, finally established in 1335.

It was not until nearly twenty years later that the most famous of these conspiracies against the oligarchy broke out—that of the Doge Marino Faliero. He is said definitely to have attempted to make the Dogeship hereditary in his family. The whole affair is obscure, but the following is the traditional account of it in Venice :

On the eleventh day of September, in the year of Our Lord 1354, Marino Faliero was elected and chosen to be the Doge of the Commonwealth of Venice. He was Count of Valdemarino, in the Marches of Treviso, and a Knight, and a wealthy man to boot. As soon as the election was completed, it was resolved in the Great Council that a deputation of twelve should be despatched to Marino Faliero the Doge,

30

who was then on his way from Rome ; for when he was chosen he was Ambassador at the Court of the Holy Father at Rome—the Holy Father himself held his Court at Avignon. When Messer Marino Faliero the Doge was about to land in Venice, on the 5th of October, 1354, a thick haze came on and darkened the air, and he was forced to land in the Piazza of S. Mark, between the two columns, on the spot where evil-doers are put to death ; and all thought that this was the worst of tokens. Nor must it be forgotten that when Messer Marino Faliero was Podestà and Captain of Treviso, the Bishop delayed coming in with the Holy Sacrament on a day when a procession was to take place. Now, the said Marino Faliero was so very proud and wrathful, that he buffeted the Bishop and almost struck him to the ground ; and, therefore, Heaven allowed Marino Faliero to go out of his right senses, in order that he might bring himself to an evil death.

When this Doge had held the Dogeship during nine months and six days, he, being wicked and ambitious, sought to make himself Lord of Venice. When the Thursday arrived upon which they were wont to hunt the bull, the bull hunt took place as usual ; and, according to the usage of those times, after the bull hunt had ended, they all proceeded unto the palace of the Doge and assembled together in one of his halls ; and they disported themselves with the women. And until the first bell tolled they danced, and then a banquet was served up. My Lord the Doge paid the expenses thereof, provided he had a Dogaressa, and after the banquet they all returned to their homes.

Now to this feast there came a certain Ser Michele Steno, a gentle-man of poor estate and very young, but crafty and daring, and who loved one of the damsels of the Dogaressa. Ser Michele stood amongst

31

the women upon the *solajo ;* and he behaved indiscreetly, so that my Lord the Doge ordered that he should be kicked off the *solajo ;* and the esquires of the Doge flung him down from the *solajo* accordingly. Ser Michele thought that such an affront was beyond all bearing ; and when the feast was over, and all other persons had left the palace, he, continuing heated with anger, went to the Hall of Audience and wrote certain unseemly words relating to the Doge and the Dogaressa upon the chair in which the Doge was used to sit ; for in those days the Doge did not cover his chair with cloth of sendal, but he sat in a chair of wood. Ser Michele wrote thereon : " Marin Falier, the husband of the fair wife ; others kiss her, but he keeps her." In the morning the words were seen, and the matter was considered to be very scandalous ; and the Senate commanded the *Avogadori*, in order to discover who had written these words. And at length it was known that Michele Steno had written them. It was resolved in the Council of Forty that he should be arrested ; and he then confessed that in the fit of vexation and spite, occasioned by his being thrust off the *solajo* in the presence of his mistress, he had written the words. Therefore the Council debated thereon. And the Council took his youth into consideration, and that he was a lover ; and therefore they adjudged that he should be kept in close confinement during two months, and that afterwards he should be banished from Venice and the State during one year. In consequence of this merciful sentence the Doge became exceedingly wroth, it appearing to him that the Council had not acted in such a manner as was required by the respect due to his ducal dignity ; and he said that they ought to have condemned Ser Michele to be hanged by the neck, or at least to be banished for life.

32

Now it was fated that my Lord Doge Marino was to have his head cut off. And as it is necessary, when any effect is to be brought about, that the cause of such effect must happen, it therefore came to pass that on the very day after sentence had been pronounced on Ser Michele Steno, being the first day of Lent, a gentleman of the house of Barbaro, a choleric gentleman, went to the arsenal and required certain things of the masters of the galleys. This he did in the presence of the Admiral of the arsenal, and he, hearing the request, answered : " No, it cannot be done." High words arose between the gentleman and the Admiral, and the gentleman struck him with his fist just above the eye ; and as he happened to have a ring on his finger, the ring cut the Admiral and drew blood. The Admiral, all bruised and bloody, ran straight to the Doge to complain, and with the intent of praying him to inflict some heavy punishment upon the gentleman of Ca Barbaro. " What wouldst thou have us do for thee ? " answered the Doge. " Think upon the shameful gibe which hath been written concerning me ; and think on the manner in which they have punished that ribald Michele Steno, who wrote it ; and see how the Council of Forty respect our person." Upon this the Admiral answered : " My Lord Doge, if you would wish to make yourself a prince, and to cut all those cuckoldy gentlemen to pieces, I have the heart, if you do but help me, to make you Prince of all this State ; and then you may punish them all." Hearing this, the Doge said : " How can such a matter be brought about ? " And so they discoursed thereon.

The Doge called for his nephew, Ser Bertuccio Faliero, who lived with him in the palace, and they communed about this plot. And without leaving the place, they sent for Philip Calendaro, a seaman of great repute,

and for Bertuccio Israello, who was exceedingly wily and cunning. Then taking counsel amongst themselves, they agreed to call in some others ; and so, for several nights successively, they met with the Doge at home in his palace. And the following men were called in singly, to wit, Niccolò Faggiuolo, Giovanni da Corfù, Stefano Fagiono, Niccolò dalle Bende, Niccolò Biondo, and Stefan Trevisano. It was concerted that sixteen or seventeen leaders should be stationed in various parts of the city, each being at the head of forty men, armed and prepared ; but the followers were not to know their destination. On the appointed day they were to make affrays amongst themselves, here and there, in order that the Doge might have a pretence for tolling the bells of San Marco ; these bells are never rung but by the order of the Doge. And at the sound of the bells, these sixteen or seventeen, with their followers, were to come to San Marco, through the streets which open upon the Piazza. And when the noble and leading citizens should come into the Piazza, to know the cause of the riot, then the conspirators were to cut them in pieces ; and this work being finished, my Lord Marino Faliero the Doge was to be proclaimed the Lord of Venice. Things having been thus settled, they agreed to fulfil their intent on Wednesday, the 15th day of April, in the year 1355. So covertly did they plot, that no one ever dreamt of their machinations.

But the Lord, who hath always helped this most glorious city, and who, loving its righteousness and holiness, hath never forsaken it, inspired one Beltramo Bergamasco to be the cause of bringing the plot to light in the following manner. This Beltramo, who belonged to Ser Niccolò Lioni of Santo Stefano, had heard a word or two of what was to take place ; and so, in the above-mentioned month of April, he went to the house of

34

the aforesaid Ser Niccolò Lioni, and told him all the particulars of the plot. Ser Niccolò, when he heard all these things, was struck dead, as it were, with affright. He heard all the particulars, and Beltramo prayed him to keep it all secret; and if he told Ser Niccolò, it was in order that Ser Niccolò might stop at home on the 15th of April, and thus save his life. Beltramo was going, but Ser Niccolò ordered his servants to lay hands upon him, and lock him up. Ser Niccolò then went to the house of Messer Giovanni Gradenigo Nasoni, who afterwards became Doge, and who also lived at Santo Stefano, and told him all. The matter seemed to him to be of the very greatest importance, as indeed it was; and they two went to the house of Ser Marco Cornaro, who lived at San Felice, and, having spoken with him, they all three then determined to go back to the house of Ser Niccolò Lioni to examine the said Beltramo; and having questioned him and heard all that he had to say they left him in confinement. And then they all three went into the sacristy of San Salvatore and sent their men to summon the Councillors, the *Avogadori*, the *Capi dei Dieci*, and those of the Great Council.

When all were assembled, the whole story was told to them. They were struck dead, as it were, with affright. They determined to send for Beltramo. He was brought in before them. They examined him, and ascertained that the matter was true, and, although they were exceedingly troubled, yet they determined upon their measures. And they sent for the *Capi de' Quarante*, the *Signori di Notte*, the *Capi de' Sestieri*, and the *Cinque della Pace*; and they were ordered to associate to their men other good men and true, who were to proceed to the houses of the ringleaders of the conspiracy and secure them. And they secured the foreman of the arsenal in order that the conspirators might not do

35

mischief. Towards nightfall they assembled in the palace. When they were assembled in the palace they caused the gates of the quadrangle of the palace to be shut. And they went to the keeper of the Bell-tower and forbade the tolling of the bells. All this was carried into effect. The before-mentioned conspirators were secured, and they were brought to the palace; and, as the Council of Ten saw that the Doge was in the plot, they resolved that twenty of the leading men of the State should be associated to them, for the purpose of consultation and deliberation, but that they should not be allowed to ballot.

The councillors were the following: Ser Giovanni Mocenigo, of the Sestiero of San Marco; Ser Almoro Veniero de Santa Marina, of the Sestiere of Castello; Ser Tomaso Viadro, of the Sestiero of Canaregio; Ser Giovanni Sanudo, of the Sestiero of Santa Croce; Ser Pietro Trivi-sano of the Sestiero of San Paolo; Ser Pantalione Barbo il Grande, of the Sestiero of Dorsoduro. The *Avogadori* of the Commonwealth were Zufredo Morosini and Ser Orio Pasqualigo; and these did not ballot. Those of the Council of Ten were Ser Giovanni Marcello, Ser Tomaso Sanudo, and Ser Micheletto Dolfino, the heads of the aforesaid Council of Ten. Ser Luca da Legge and Ser Pietro da Mosto, inquisitors of the aforesaid Council, and Ser Marco Polani, Ser Marino Veniero, Ser Lando Lombardo, and Ser Nicoletto Trivisano, of Sant' Angelo.

Late in the night, just before the dawning, they chose a junta of twenty noblemen of Venice from amongst the wisest, and the worthiest, and the oldest. They were to give counsel, but not to ballot. And they would not admit anyone of Ca Faliero. And Niccolò Faliero, and another Niccolò Faliero, of San Tomaso, were expelled from the Council, because

36

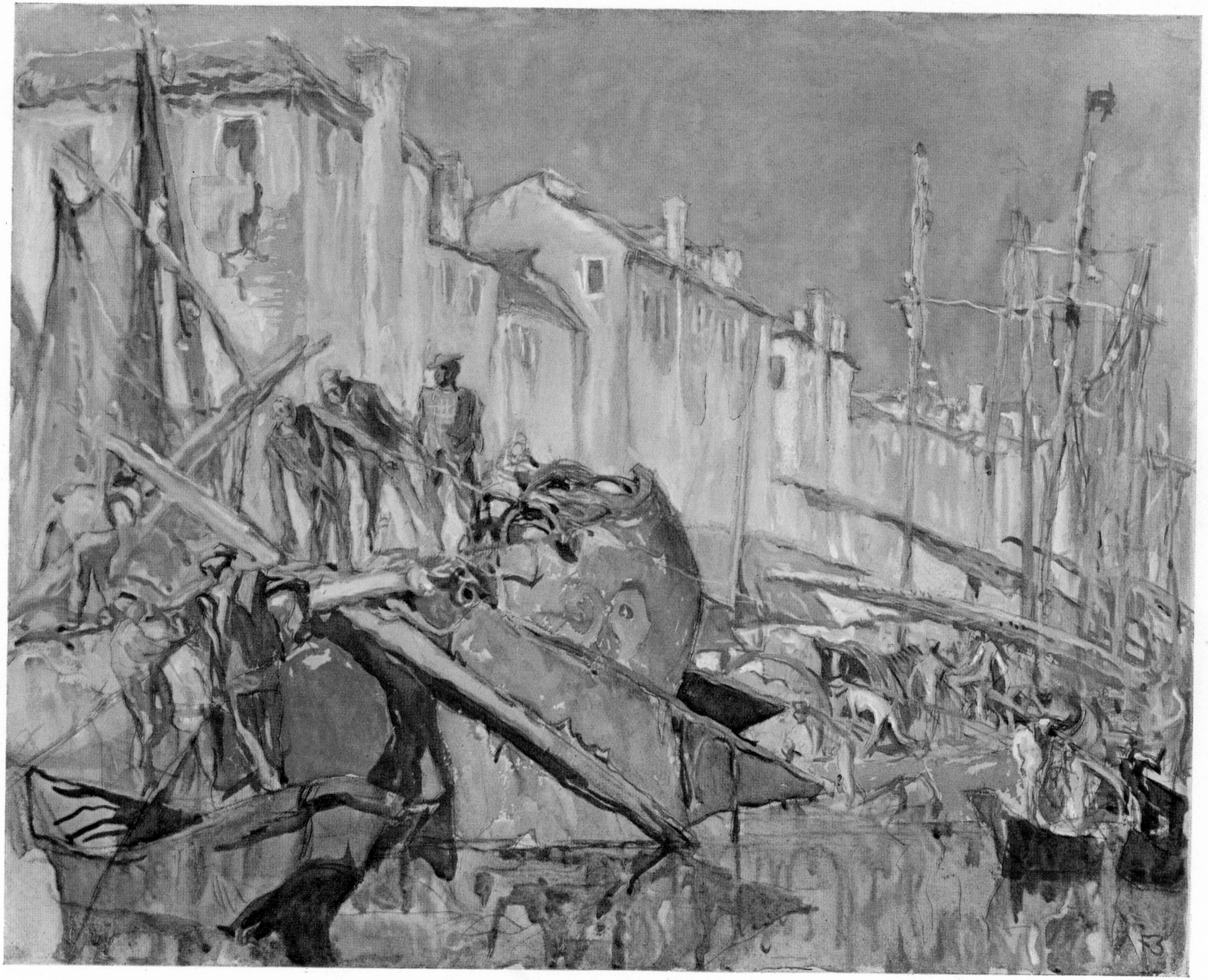

"BOATS FROM THE MAINLAND"

they belonged to the family of the Doge. And this resolution of creating the junta of twenty was much praised throughout the State.

These twenty men were accordingly called in to the Council of Ten; and they sent for my Lord Marino Faliero the Doge; and my Lord Marino was then consorting in the palace with people of great estate, gentlemen, and other good men, none of whom knew yet how the fact stood.

At the same time Bertucci Israello, who, as one of the ringleaders, was to head the conspirators in Santa Croce, was arrested and bound, and brought before the Council. Zanello del Brin, Nicoletto di Rosa, Nicoletto Alberto, and the Guardiaga were also taken, together with several seamen, and people of various ranks. These were examined, and the truth of the plot was ascertained.

On the 16th of April judgment was given in the Council of Ten, that Filippo Calendaro and Bertuccio Israello should be hanged upon the red pillars of the balcony of the palace, from which the Doge is wont to look at the bull hunt : and they were hanged with gags in their mouths.

The next day the nine others were condemned. These were all taken at Chioggia, for they were endeavouring to escape. Afterwards, by virtue of the sentence which was passed upon them in the Council of Ten, they were hanged on successive days, some singly and some in couples, upon the columns of the palace, beginning from the red columns, and so going onwards towards the canal. And other prisoners were discharged because, although they had been involved in the conspiracy, yet they had not assisted in it, for they were given to understand by some of the heads of the plot that they were to come armed and prepared for the service of the State, and in order to secure certain criminals, and they knew

37

nothing else. Nicoletto Alberto, the Guardiaga, and Bartolommeo Ciricolo and his son, and several others, who were not guilty, were discharged.

On Friday, the 16th day of April, judgment was also given in the aforesaid Council of Ten, that my Lord Marino Faliero the Doge should have his head cut off, and that the execution should be done on the landing-place of the stone staircase, where the Doges take their oath when they first enter the palace. On the following day, the 17th of April, the doors of the palace being shut, the Doge had his head cut off about the hour of noon. And the cap of estate was taken from the Doge's head before he came downstairs. When the execution was over, it is said that one of the Council of Ten went to the columns of the palace over against the Piazza of S. Mark, and that he shewed the bloody sword unto the people, crying out with a loud voice, "The terrible doom hath fallen upon the traitor!" and the doors were opened, and the people all rushed in to see the corpse of the Doge who had been beheaded.

It must be known that Ser Giovanni Sanudo, the councillor, was not present when the aforesaid sentence was pronounced, because he was unwell and remained at home. So that only fourteen balloted, that is to say, five councillors and nine of the Council of Ten. And it was adjudged that all the lands and chattels of the Doge, as well as of the other traitors, should be forfeited to the State. And as a grace to the Doge, it was resolved in the Council of Ten that he should be allowed to dispose of two thousand ducats out of his own property. And it was resolved that all the councillors and all the *Avogadori* of the Commonwealth, those of the Council of Ten and the members of the junta who had assisted in passing sentence on the Doge and the other traitors, should have the

38

privilege of carrying arms both by day and by night in Venice, and from Grado to Cavazere. And they were also to be allowed two footmen carrying arms, the aforesaid footmen living and boarding with them in their own homes. And he who did not keep two footmen might transfer the privilege to his sons or his brothers; but only to two. Permission of carrying arms was also granted to the four Notaries of the Chancery, that is to say, of the Supreme Court, who took the depositions, and to the secretaries of the *Signori di Notte*.

After the traitors had been hanged, and the Doge had had his head cut off, the State remained in great tranquillity and peace. And the corpse of the Doge was removed in a barge, with eight torches, to his tomb in the church of SS. Giovanni e Paolo, where it was buried. The tomb is now in that aisle in the middle of the little church of Santa Maria della Pace, which was built by Bishop Gabriel of Bergamo. It is a coffin of stone, with these words engraven thereon, " HIC JACET DOMINUS MARINUS FALETRO DUX." And they did not paint his portrait in the hall of the Great Council, but in the place where it ought to have been you see these words, " HIC EST LOCUS MARINI FALETRO, DECAPITATI PRO CRIMINIBUS." And it is thought that his house was granted to the church of Sant' Apostoli; it was that great one near the bridge. Yet this could not be the case, or else the family bought it back from the church, for it still belongs to Ca Faliero.

V

# VENICE IN THE FOURTEENTH CENTURY.

THESE conspiracies, as I have said, seem to fill the fourteenth century in Venice ; but it would be a mistake to imagine that politics, either internal or external, occupy a great part in the life of a people ruled by an oligarchy. Venice was always a city of merchants ; shipping was her greater business and the trade it involved, and we shall miss altogether the splendour of the time if we fix our attention either upon foreign affairs or internal convulsion. The real energy of the State, and the lives of nine out of ten of its inhabitants were very far from such things. They were given to business, to shipbuilding, to merchant adventures, to glass-making and lace-making and fishing, and a thousand activities for the amassing of money and winning a livelihood. It is indeed now that the great groups of artists and craftsmen appear to develop with extraordinary rapidity into formidable societies controlling the various energies in production throughout the city State.

Perhaps the most famous of these crafts, apart from that of the *Arsenalotti*, of which we have already spoken, was the art of the glass blowers, which brought so much wealth and so much fame to Venice. Beside the Libro d'Oro there had, in this city of burghers, been established a Silver Book, and therein were inscribed the names of citizens " de jure." In this book the names of all the glass makers of Murano were written from birth, for they were considered as benefactors of the State. So valuable was this craft thought to be to the State that later it was enacted that even an attempt at emigration on the part of a glass maker should be punishable by death. Thus for centuries Venice remained the headquarters of this manufacture, and indeed kept the trade almost entirely in her own hands. Murano was the centre of the craft, and in the days of its greatness, from the fourteenth century onwards, Murano was not only one of the most famous, but one of the most beautiful cities of the lagoon. As early as the fifteenth century it had no less than 30,000 inhabitants, most of them engaged in this business, and though to-day it has a population of but 5000 it still manufactures glass, and you may see the heirs of the old great craftsmen wielding the blowing-irons while, inspired by their breath, the molten glass swells and twists and divides into a thousand fantastic and beautiful shapes. Alas, the more lovely things are no longer made. Where are the famous mirrors, or the beakers and glasses so fine, so light, of so rare a purity and quality, that it was said they would burst into fragments if so much as a drop of poison was poured into them ?

But it was not only in the rise of such crafts as this and the establishment of the greater guilds that the life of Venice was remarkable at this time. Everything was changing, the customs not less than the aspect of a place which was quickly becoming one of the great cities and powers of the world.

G

For instance, it is at this time we find the old customs with regard to marriage, so fundamental a thing as that, passing away.

It had been the custom in Venice for all marriages to take place on the same day, the second of February, the Feast of the Purification, or Candlemas, and in the same church, the old Cathedral of Venice, S. Pietro d'Olivolo or di Castello, and this custom gave rise to a national festa called the *Festa dei Matrimoni o delle Marie*. The girls about to be married presented themselves there with their poor little dots in a little *cassa* called *arcella*. There they awaited their future husbands, who arrived accompanied by their parents, their friends, and a crowd of spectators. All assisted at the Mass celebrated by the Bishop, who preached a sermon on the sanctity of the engagements that were about to be contracted, and on the duties that God imposed upon married people. He then gave the episcopal benediction to each couple. When the ceremonies were completed the husbands gave their hands to their wives and, having received the *arcelle*, returned home amid the joyous crowd that had accompanied them to the church.

Later, when the Venetian constitution was enacted and fixed and the city was full of riches and overflowing with population, it was decided to render this ceremony more brilliant and splendid. It was decreed that twelve girls of irreproachable conduct and of especial beauty, drawn from among the poorest in the city, should receive dots from the State and go to the altar accompanied by the Doge himself, in his ducal mantle and followed by his suite. The brides, however, still went simply dressed in white, wearing a white veil, but their hair was ornamented in as rich a manner as possible with pearls and diamonds, and crowned with a golden crown. These ornaments were provided by the State and surrendered again after the ceremony.

But what gave this festa its special and national character was the memory of one of the most amazing events that befell the city in the tenth century. In the year 944, during this ceremony, certain Dalmatian pirates suddenly descended upon Venice and attempted at once to possess themselves of a goodly booty of money and jewels, and of many fair women who might be sold for a good price or kept as slaves. In fact they succeeded and carried off the brides. But they had reckoned without the Venetians, who, with the Doge at their head, set off in pursuit. Every boat was manned, and a tremendous race began. The wind failed, and pursuers and pursued took to their oars, and the Venetians found themselves the better men, for they caught the Dalmatians and slew every one of them, and brought the little brides back to Venice unharmed.

The Venetians wished this should be for ever remembered, and as the carpenters had furnished and manned the greatest number of boats on this occasion, they were allowed to choose their recompense. They asked that the Doge should visit their parish on the day of the festival. The Doge, surprised at their naive modesty, asked, " And if it should rain ? " " We will give you hats to cover yourselves." " And if we should be thirsty ? " " We will give you to drink." And so to the last days of the Republic the Doge, with the Signoria, every year on the Feast of the Purification visited the Church of S. Maria Formosa and he and the Signoria were presented with hats of straw and with flasks of wine and oranges.

It seems to have been this ceremony that, perhaps, after the old custom of all marriages being celebrated on the same day in the same

43

church had passed away, gave the name of the *Festa delle Marie* to the festival instead of the *Festa dei Matrimoni*. This festa then came to fill not one day but eight, and was famous throughout Italy. During those eight days the twelve young women proceeded through all Venice. Each day offered a new spectacle. The girls, sumptuously dressed by the State, went first in boats finely adorned to visit the Doge, then to the patriarchal church to give thanks for the ancient victory over the pirates, accompanying the Doge. Then they proceeded to S. Mark's, where he bid them farewell, and shewed the assembled people " The Maries," as the girls were called ; then re-embarked and made the voyage up the Grand Canal, hung with tapestries for the occasion and full of music. Everywhere they received gifts. But by the middle of the fourteenth century the earlier simplicity had passed away, and it became necessary to substitute figures of wood for the girls in the procession, and by 1379 the whole festival was suppressed for ever, except the visit of the Doge to S. Maria Formosa.

I have said that people came from all over Italy in the fourteenth century to take part in this festival. In truth Venice was already become what she has ever since remained, a joy city for all Europe. There were many inns for the stranger, such as the *Luna*, the *Leone Bianco*, or the *Selvatico*, just as there are still, and a certain supervision was even then exercised over them.

Perhaps the two most famous strangers who visited Venice at this time were Petrarch and Boccaccio. It was there in 1363 in the house in the Schiavone that Boccaccio brought Pilatus, who was translating Homer for him for the first time, to visit Petrarch, to whom Boccaccio was wholly devoted. It was a notable meeting, and that it gave Petrarch as much

44

pleasure as it gave Boccaccio consolation, we know from his letters. Four years later he came to see Petrarch in Venice again, but found him absent. This visit Boccaccio records in one of the most delightful of his letters. On the way from Florence he met Petrarch's son-in-law, whose character, voice and beauty he praises so highly. "After further and friendly greetings," he writes to Petrarch, "after hearing from him that you were safe and sound, and much other good news concerning you, I began to consider him. . . . Finally he left me. . . . And I in the earliest dawn went aboard my little boat and immediately set out for the Venetian shore, where I landed, and would have sent at once to announce myself, but some of our brother citizens were already about me and offering me hospitality. . . . In spite, however, of Donato's pressing invitation, I went off with Frencesco Allegri. . . . I tell you all this in all these words to excuse myself for not having accepted the offer you made me so warmly by letter ; but if my friends had not been there to meet me I should have gone to an inn rather than have dwelt in the house of Tullia[1] while her husband was absent. However, although you know in this and in many other things the integrity of my heart towards you, all others would not know it, and some would have jeered in spite of my white head and my age and my fatness and feebleness which should surely shut their mouths. This kind of thing is easily and willingly believed by evil-minded scandalmongers who prefer a lie to the truth.

"After reposing myself a little I went to salute Tullia, who had already heard of my arrival. . . . She met me joyfully, blushing a little and looking on the ground with modesty and filial affection, and she saluted and embraced me. . . .

[1] Petrarch's daughter.

45

" Presently we were talking in your charming little garden with some friends, and she offered me with matronly serenity your house, your books, and all your things there. Suddenly little footsteps—and there came towards us thy Eletta, my delight, who without knowing who I was looked at me smiling. I was not only delighted, I greedily took her in my arms, imagining that I held my little one[1] who is lost to me. What shall I say ? If you do not believe me you will believe Guglielmo da Ravenna, the physician, and our Donato, who knew her. Your little one has the same aspect that she had who was my Eletta, the same expression, the same light in the eyes, the same laughter there, the same gestures, the same way of walking, the same way of carrying all her little person ; only my Eletta was, it is true, a little taller when at the age of five and a half I saw her for the last time. Besides, she talks in the same way, uses the same words, and has the same simplicity. Indeed, indeed, there is no difference save that thy little one is golden haired, while mine had chestnut tresses. Ah me ! How many times when I have held thine in my arms, listening to her prattle, the memory of my baby, stolen away from me, has brought tears to my eyes—which I let no one see."

That love of children, so characteristic in an Italian, and yet so surprising in Boccaccio to those who, without understanding the real simplicity of his nature, have been content to think of him as a mere teller of doubtful stories, is one of the most natural and beautiful traits in his character. The little Eletta, " my delight," appears like a ray of sunshine in his lonely and sombre old age which we may think, perhaps, had

[1] It is of his little daughter Violante he speaks, who died, as he says, " at an age when one goes straight to heaven."

46

Violante lived, might have been less bitter, less hard to bear than it proved to be.

Petrarch seems to have had a real love for Venice. He had been there first on embassy and sought it again as a refuge from the plague. It was while there that Boccaccio offered to sell him his library, and though this never came about, Petrarch drew up then a memorandum, indeed an irrevocable deed, assigning all his own books to the Republic of Venice after his death. Whether this deed was ever signed we do not know, but certainly as an acknowledgment the Palazzo Molin was assigned to him on the Schiavoni. These books never came to Venice, however, and they did not form the nucleus of the Marcian Library, as visitors are told, even to-day. The real nucleus of that famous collection was the library of Cardinal Bessarion in the fifteenth century. What became of Petrarch's books we do not know, but some of them are now in Paris and others scattered in various libraries on the Continent.

That Petrarch was devoted to Venice in his later years, in spite of his earlier partisanship for Genoa, is certain. He writes of her as " the most august city of Venice the one remaining home of liberty, peace and justice, the one refuge left to good men, the one harbour where the ships of those who desire to live worthily may still find shelter from war. This city is rich in gold but richer still in reputation ; strong in resources, stronger in worth, founded on marble yet set on a more solid foundation of civil peace ; safeguarded by the salt encircling sea, but safeguarded still more by the salt of good counsel." Indeed, in the chaos of the world at that time Venice must have appeared the only refuge, the only solid thing left in a world in dissolution. And it is Petrarch from his window on the Riva who gives us the best picture of Venice at this time. " From my window," he writes, " I see ships as large as my house with masts taller than its towers.  They sail to every part of the world, and face a thousand dangers.  They carry wine to England, honey to the Black Sea, saffron, oil and linen to Assyria, Armenia, Persia, and Arabia ;  wood to Egypt and Greece, and they return laden with merchandise from all Europe. And where the sea ends their sailors leave their ships and travel overland to trade in India and China ;  they traverse the Caucasus and the Ganges, and so on even to the Eastern Ocean."

We cannot leave the fourteenth century, politically perhaps the greatest for Venice of all that go to make up her long life, without glancing, however cursorily, at the fundamental changes in her policy which then began and which filled the whole of the fifteenth century.  From an island, Venice became a great continental power.  Economically this was as necessary to her as it was politically.

It was in 1339 that she became a continental power with a land frontier as easily attacked as any other ;  till then she had been an impregnable island holding the sea which was her frontier.

## VI

## VENICE IN THE FIFTEENTH CENTURY.

VENICE was, as we know, above all a great mercantile State; for the distribution of her merchandise from the East and from all the Eastern Mediterranean she needed the roads behind her up to the Alps. Should these be in the hands of an enemy her business could be, as indeed it had been more than once, killed by duties and tariffs. Nor was this all. She needed territory, for the sake of production. She could not feed herself with her growing population from the islands and mud-banks of the lagoon. She could be blockaded, as she knew, and if an enemy behind her held the mainland she could be starved into surrender. These, much more than any political ambitions, were the causes that determined her expansion upon *terra firma*.

We cannot here go into the details of this long business of land war and conquest, nor relate how she achieved so great a revolution in her policy, raising an army by universal service and overthrowing the Carrara of Padua, the Scala of Verona, and facing the Visconti of Milan. By the

H

first years of the fifteenth century all had been accomplished; the ancient frontiers of the province of Venetia were restored, and Venice ruled from the Alps to the Po, from the sea to Lago di Garda and the Mincio, and continued to rule there for four hundred years. She then appeared as one of the great States of Europe, far richer and more stable than any other government in Italy, and to outlast them all, except the Papacy.

And so it is that if the fourteenth century passes us by in Venice like some great naval pageant, splendid with ships and fleets and resounding with the names of great admirals, the fifteenth seems to pass in a military pageant, filled with the rumour of the fame of great *condottieri*, those soldiers of fortune, almost princes, in the pay of the great maritime republic, Carmagnola, Gattamelata, Francesco Sforza, Bartolommeo Colleoni, Roberto Sanseverino and such. And two of them at least she commemorates in two of the great equestrian statues in the world—Gattamelata in Padua from the hand of Donatello, Bartolommeo Colleoni in Venice itself from the hand of Andrea Verrocchio. This last, which still stands in the Piazza di SS. Giovanni e Paolo, for which it was designed, was the last work of that great master. Vasari tells us the story of its creation. " The Venetians," says he, " at this time, desiring to do honour to the distinguished valour of Bartolommeo da Bergamo (Colleoni) who had obtained for them many great victories, resolved to raise a monument to his name, hoping thereby to encourage other leaders. Having heard the renown of Andrea, they therefore invited him to Venice, where he was commissioned to execute an equestrian statue of the commander above named, which was to be placed on the Piazza of SS. Giovanni e Paolo. The master accordingly having prepared the model, was proceeding to take the necessary measures for casting it in bronze when, by the

50

"S. MARIA DEI FRARI"

favour of certain persons among the Venetian nobles, it was determined that Vellano of Padua should execute the figure of the general, and Andrea Verrocchio that of the horse only; but the latter no sooner heard this than, having first broken the head and legs of his model, he returned in great anger to Florence, without saying a word. This departure being told to the Signoria, they caused him to understand that he should never dare again to enter Venice, for if he did so they would take off his head. To this menace the master wrote in reply that he would take care not to return, seeing that when they had once taken off his head it would be beyond their power to give him another, nor could they ever get as good a one put on the horse, whose head he had broken, as he would have made for it. Notwithstanding this reply, which did not displease those nobles, Andrea was afterwards induced to return to Venice, when his appointments were doubled. He then restored his first model and cast it in bronze, but did not entirely finish it, for having taken cold when he had exposed himself to much fatigue and heat in casting the work, he died in Venice after a few days' illness."

These great works of art, of their sort the greatest in the world, were created for the Venetians in the fifteenth century; but they were the work of Tuscan artists, for Venice had no one capable of producing such works of her own. Indeed Venice was much later in developing a school of art of her own than either Tuscany or Umbria. Not till the appearance of the Bellini in the fifteenth century did she produce any painters of first-rate ability, and when the Venetian school does at length appear it is an essentially different thing from the school of Florence or the school of Siena, already so famous throughout the peninsula. Yet different, essentially different, though it be, it is by no means less glorious. Indeed,

51

in many respects it surpassed every other school in Italy, and finally must perhaps be regarded as the greatest school of painting of which we have any record.

The Venetian school of painting which thus occupies so great a place in the history of European art may be said really to declare itself with the work of the Bellini, out of whom came all the great masters of the sixteenth century. It is thus nearly two hundred years later in its origin than the schools of Florence and Siena. Venice has no Cimabue or Giotto, no Duccio at all. These masters of the thirteenth and early fourteenth centuries in Florence and Siena were the giants who decided the whole future of painting in Tuscany, and they were the children of their time.

The Florentine and the Sienese schools of painting, the schools of Giotto and Duccio, were chiefly concerned with religion. The greatest works of the masters of these schools were produced for the Church and for the most part consist of frescoes to decorate a nave or sanctuary or a chapel, or of altar-pieces which in various forms stood over the altar and were part of the furniture of religion. The Venetian school on the contrary had little to do with religion—it is the first and perhaps the only secular school in Italy. It was, as we shall see, not the Church, but the State which inspired it and which it served, and it differed essentially, too, from the two schools of Tuscany not only thus in its condition but in its intention also ; its main technical characteristic is not the nobility and integrity of its drawing, nor the beauty and delight of its decoration, but the splendour of its colour, its occupation with the gestures and joy of life. Perhaps what is meant will be clearer if put in another way. It is Giotto who decides, once and for all, what the condition and intention

52

of the Florentine school of painting shall be ; his mind and his work are inherent in all the Florentine masters who come after him, except perhaps in Botticelli. It is Duccio who decides once and for all what the condition and intention of Sienese painting shall be ; it is his mind and his work which are inherent in all the Sienese masters who come after him, till we come to Sodoma, who is not properly Sienese at all and for that very reason. It is not Florence, the city and State of Florence which produces the Florentine school, it is Giotto. It is not Siena, the city and State of Siena which produces the Sienese school, it is Duccio. But it is not any master or masters—not the Bellini even—who produce and inspire and define the Venetian school, it is Venice and the city and State of Venice. Venice was more than a State, she was a nation, the only nation in Italy, and she produced the first national school of painting in the modern world.

We note, and we are right to note, that the work of Masaccio, of Michaelangelo even, is implicit in the work of Giotto. We note, and we are right to note, that the work of Sassetta, for instance, is implicit in the work of Duccio. Can we say the same of the work of Giorgione, of Titian, of Tintoretto, of Paolo Veronese ? These masters owe something, even much, to Giovanni Bellini, but can we say that their work is implicit in the work of that master ? We cannot. Each of these great painters, and Giovanni Bellini too, is an absolutely new impulse in painting. Fundamentally they owe nothing to their predecessors even though, accidentally, they owe much. They are not prophesied of, they prophesy ; they are each of them great and original creators, as we say, in painting, and together they make up a school which is Venetian, because each and all of these masters owe everything not to any predecessor but to Venice ;

53

and to this school, to them, that is, all the later masters of Europe, save Rembrandt, appeal; Velasquez as well as Rubens, Vandyck as well as Reynolds.

The Venetian school of Painting which appeared thus in the fifteenth century, with the Bellini, Jacopo Bellini (active 1430–70), the pupil of Gentile da Fabriano the Umbrian and Pisanello the Veronese; and his sons Gentile and Giovanni; was a national school, the production chiefly of Venice, which, to the end, it served rather than the Church. It is peculiar in these two things as a school: it is wholly national and it is civic rather than religious. There is not in all Venice, or indeed outside Venice, a series of frescoes or pictures by a Venetian master which can be put beside the work of Giotto in S. Croce or at Assisi, or of Ghirlandajo in S. Maria Novella. These were great religious *storie* painted in the service of religion; but the one series of pictures from a Venetian hand which leaps to the mind in comparison, the pictures by Carpaccio in S. Giorgio degli Schiavoni, were not painted in the service of religion, but in a " national " Church, in the service of " nationalism "; for the Dalmatians, whose national Church this was, and whose national saint was S. George. Moreover, it is not in the churches of Venice that you will find, if at all, anything that may be put beside the great fresco sequences of the Tuscan and Umbrian painters, but in the Doge's Palace where not less than three series of paintings have been destroyed and replaced by the glorious work we see, and in the *Scuole*, and in the guild houses of the great secular guilds; not in the Frari, the Franciscan Church, or in SS. Giovanni e Paolo, the Dominican Church, where we might expect to find them, but in the Scuola di S. Rocco and the Scuola di S. Maria della Carità, the meeting houses of lay guilds.

54

The Venetian school was thus pre-eminently a national school, influenced chiefly by Venice, its life and landscape; and it was civic, not religious; it served not the Church but the State. Glorious with famous names that fill the sixteenth century with its fame, it begins properly in the fifteenth century with the work of the Bellini, and does not pass away till Venice herself is about to die. Her great painters pass down the centuries of her glory and her decline like an army with banners. Jacopo and Gentile and Giovanni Bellini, Vittore Carpaccio, Cima, Catena, Bissolo, Basaiti, Giorgione of Castelfranco, Sebastiano del Piombo, Palma Vecchio, Titian, Tintoretto, Paolo Veronese, Pietro Longhi, Tiepolo, Canaletto, Guardi. If the first saw Wendelin di Spira set up his printing press in Venice, the last heard the reverberation of the Revolution over the Alps.

We should find it difficult to obtain a picture of Florence or Siena from the pictures of the Florentine or Sienese painters, but the works of the Venetians are full of Venice. Thus Gentile Bellini paints for us the Piazza di S. Marco in the Procession of the Holy Cross, the canals of Venice in the Finding of the Relic; Sebastiano and Mansueti continue the series. With Giorgione we begin a marvellous gallery of Venetian landscapes, while Titian and Tintoret give us an innumerable portraiture of Doges, nobles, men of letters and fair women. With Veronese we pass through the courtyards and galleries of the Palaces of Venice, with Longhi we see the interior life of the town, while Canaletto paints the whole landscape of the city and Guardi the canals and the lagoons.

But it was not only in the art of painting that Venice was to begin to excel in the fifteenth century. Far more famous than her achievement

55

in the major art at this time was her reputation in the minor art of printing, and here too, for all her fame, she was not an originator.

That her share was very large in that revolutionary achievement of printing from movable type is true, but it was not in Venice or even in Italy that the art was invented.  It was Germany that here led the way : nor was Venice, according to the best opinion, the first city in Italy to produce a printed book.  That honour belongs neither to Venice nor to an Italian.  It was the Germans, Sweynheym and Pannartz, who produced the first book printed in Italy, in the year 1465, and in Subiaco. It is true that priority has been claimed for Venice and for the famous Frenchman, Nicholas Jenson, who, according to the colophon of the *Decor Puellarum*, printed that book in Venice in Roman type in the year 1461.  But modern opinion is almost universally agreed now that the date which appears in that work MCCCCLXI is a misprint for MCCCCLXXI, that is to say 1471, an error arising from the omission of the Roman numeral X.  The first book printed in Venice is therefore not Nicholas Jenson's *Decor Puellarum* but John di Spira's *Epistolæ Familiares*, printed in 1469.  This being so, Venice has to give precedence not only to Subiaco but to Rome as the cradle of printing in Italy.

Printing was thus introduced into Venice by John of Spira—Speier in Bavaria—and his brother Wendelin.  We know very little of them, not even the date of their arrival in Venice, but they were very well received, and John di Spira died in 1470, the year after the appearance of his first book, while the *De Civitate Dei* was in the press.  Wendelin completed this work, and recorded his brother's death in the colophon

56

"FRUIT BOATS"

of it.  The two brothers seem to have thus produced four works in about ten months : Cicero's *Epistolæ Familiares* of 1469, of which a hundred copies were printed in all in three months ;  the second edition of this, dated 1470 ;  Pliny's *De Naturali Historia* ;  and the first volume of Livy's *Historiarum Romanorum Decades.*

In 1469 John di Spira had been granted a monopoly of printing in Venice, but this seems to have lapsed with his death, and in 1470 Nicholas Jenson, the greatest of all Venetian printers, appears and issues certainly four, if not five, works : Eusebius, *De Evangelica Præparatione ;* Justinus, *Epitomata ;* Cicero, *Epistolæ ad Atticum ; Rhetorica* and *De Inventione* and perhaps Guarini, *Regulæ Grammaticæ.*  Where Jenson designed and cut his type is not known, whether he brought it to Venice with him or cut it there we shall never know, but his Roman type was incomparable, and became a sort of pattern or example which other and later printers down to our own time have attempted to equal, and never with complete success.

This is not the place to give a history of the Venetian Press, but in touching upon the glorious achievement of Venice in the fifteenth century, a few names must be mentioned.  Jenson's own work was finished in Venice by 1480 ;  and we ought to note that it is with the beginning of this second decade that works of inferior craftsmanship begin to appear. All the earlier printers are foreigners ;  but in 1472 a Venetian, Filippo di Pietro, issued an Italian work, the *Philocolo* of Boccaccio.  In 1476 Erhard Ratdolt, Bernard Pictor and Peter Loslein established their famous press, and began to issue their gloriously decorated books, which in their own way have never been surpassed, or perhaps equalled.  Their first book, as lovely in type as in decoration, was the *Calendarium* of Johann Muller,

I

with a wonderful flowered border and fine astronomical illustrations or diagrams. This book affords the earliest known example of an ornamental title page, as well as of the considerable use in Italy of woodcut initials. It does not give us quite the first use of the latter, for Wendelin di Spira, in 1471, in the Valerius Maximus *Facta et dicta*, has a large ornamental capital on the *recto* of the third leaf. However, it is Ratdolt who first produces these woodcut initials in any quantity, and it is to him we owe the marvellously lovely woodcut borders for which his books are famous. That these borders were designed and produced by Italians in Venice might seem certain. They are altogether Italian in feeling and no German, then or later, could have approached them in refinement and beauty, much less invented them.

Both Wendelin di Spira and Jenson had already produced three kinds of characters in their type, Roman, Gothic, and Greek. The Roman type was the earliest and always the most beautiful, and indeed, as I have said, as Jenson cut it has never been surpassed. The Gothic character seems to have been cut and used to save space. The first printer to use this type in Venice was Wendelin, and we find it first in 1473 in Roberto di Litio's *Quadragesimale*. In 1477 he issued a Dante in this character. Jenson began to use it in 1475 for S. Augustine's *De Civitate Dei*, which he issued in that year. This is a very lovely book.

It was, on the other hand, Jenson who first introduced Greek characters to the Venetian Press. These appear in 1471 in his edition of the *Epistolæ Familiares*. The type is very fine, and it is unfortunate that he never issued a Greek book. The first Greek book printed in Italy comes from Milan in 1476; it is Lascaris's Greek Grammar. No printer in Venice produced such a book till 1485, when Pellegrino da Bologna

58

issued Chrysoloras's *Erotomania*.   But it is not till Aldus appears that Greek books were anything but very rare.   That great scholar-craftsman, born at Sermoneta in 1450, began his career as a printer in Venice in 1494. His object was the publication of the Greek classics.   Till he appeared only four of these had been printed—Æsop, Theocritus, Homer, and Isocrates.   In 1494 he issued the *Galeomyomachia* and the Musæus : *De Heroæ et Leandro*.   In 1500 he founded his academy for the study of Greek and the production and editing of Greek books.   All the members of the Academy were bound to speak Greek among themselves, and it was thus the amazing work of producing editions of the great Greek poets and prose writers was successfully accomplished.   This alone was an almost unequalled service to humanism ; but Aldus, though his most noble work was given to Greek, also printed, and especially in handy editions, with the italic characters for which his books are famous, editions of Latin and Italian authors.   For instance, it was he who first collected and printed the poems of Lorenzo de' Medici.   Altogether the services of Aldus to learning are beyond any computation.

Why then do we find that it is in Venice these great printers—Germans, Frenchmen and Italians—set up their presses ?   In the first place, perhaps, because with the fall of Constantinople an infinite number of manuscripts found their way to Venice.   Then Venice was perhaps the greatest market in Europe, the first of all distributing centres.   And lastly, because of the excellence and cheapness of the Venetian paper.   However that may be, the Venetian Press soon appeared as the greatest in Italy, and indeed in Europe.   It was the last, and in many ways the greatest achievement of Venice in the fifteenth century, certainly the most far-reaching, and it is consoling to think of the noble city at her greatest

59

moment concerned in such an universal service : one which, if in some final catastrophe all her glorious buildings should be swept away, her noble pictures destroyed, her very ruins sunk in the Adriatic, and even her story forgotten, would for ever keep her name and her fame in the memory of man, even to the furthest generation.

## VII

## SIXTEENTH-CENTURY VENICE.

THE enormous catastrophe of the Fall of Constantinople in 1453 found Venice at her greatest. It is true that the splendour and the gaiety of the great city State continued almost to the end of the sixteenth century, but the capture of Byzantium by the Turks was, though no one at the time suspected it, almost a mortal wound. With the Turk in Europe, it fell to Venice to face him. She " was the safeguard of the West," and too often she was left to carry out that onerous task alone. It ruined and crippled her.

Upon the top of this tragedy for all Europe, came a tragedy peculiar to herself. In 1497 Vasco da Gama sailed round the Cape of Good Hope, and opened up a new route to the Indies. This was an even worse blow at her life, for soon she was to be left in the backwater of the Adriatic, while the trade of Europe passed by another road.

As though this were not enough, in 1508 the League of Cambray was formed for the purpose of " putting a stop to losses, injuries, rapine and damage which Venice had inflicted not merely on the Holy See but on the Empire, the House of Austria, the Duchy of Milan, the King of Naples, and other princes." For "wheresoever the carcase is, there will the eagles be gathered together." Venice was dying, wounded to death by all these things, and yet during the years of her long decline, for she did not die until the treaty of Campo Formio handed her over to the Empire in 1797, she was incomparable, the greatest, the noblest and the most splendid State of Italy. It was in these years that she became " the revel of the world, the masque of Italy."

Now of all the pictures and descriptions and accounts which have come down to us of Venice at this time, and they are innumerable and often from the hands of great men of letters, not one gives us so true an impression, so living an atmosphere and so complete a possession of the city of the sixteenth century as that we have from an Englishman who almost certainly never visited her. Where else in all literature are we to find so miraculous a picture of Venice as we get in *The Merchant of Venice* and in the first act of *Othello*? Where else are we so completely transferred to the city of the lagoons? And this is so obviously true that more than one heavy German is sure that Shakespeare must have been in Venice with a Baedeker and a notebook. As one of them writes : " The poetic imagination may be never so lively and creative, and the power of imitation never so highly developed ; one thing cannot be disputed, namely, that it bestows upon no one a knowledge of facts, but that such knowledge can only be acquired by experience or must be imparted by others." However that may be, it is not so much in his "facts" that Shakespeare astonishes us, as in his spirit, his complete possession of the atmosphere of the scene and movement of his play.

The " facts " indeed come to very little, indeed seem to come to little more than the use of a nonsensical word " tranect " in the following passage from *The Merchant of Venice.*

> . . . Bring them I pray thee with imagined speed
> Unto the tranect, to the common ferry
> Which trades to Venice.

Theobald restores this word to traject and the German cited would connect it with the Italian *traghetto.* Surely, supposing the correction of Theobald to have been right, and supposing the word *traghetto* ever to have been spelt *tragetto* in Venice, Shakespeare could have learned this " fact " by word of mouth from any Italian or Italianate Englishman at the Court or in the city of London. So he might have learnt that the Isola di Rialto and the Rialto Bridge were not to be confounded.

No, it is not here and in such things as these we can find delight, but rather in the whole magic picture Shakespeare gives us, as true as it is magical, of Venice and Belmont. Take for instance the marvellous Venetian night which Shakespeare alone knows how to shew us, which opens Act V of *The Merchant of Venice :*

> The moon shines bright : in such a night as this
> When the sweet wind did gently kiss the trees
> And they did make no noise. . . .

So it opens, and is absolutely perfect in its beauty and in its suggestion of Venice to the end :

> Look how the floor of heaven
> Is thick inlaid with patines of bright gold :
> There's not the smallest orb which thou behold'st

But in his motion like an angel sings,
Still quiring to the young-eyed cherubins;
Such harmony is in immortal souls;
But whilst this muddy vesture of decay
Doth grossly close it in, we cannot hear it.

These words are more than any facts : these words are poetry.

Shakespeare, who, for all the Germans may say, was in all probability never in Venice, has yet given us, as we have seen, a marvellous effect of her spirit and atmosphere. His great contemporary, Michel de Montaigne, though he was undoubtedly there in 1581, and has left us an account of his journey, gives us no sort of picture of the city.

In his Essays, Montaigne tells us that he too found Venice beautiful, and had a kindness for her. " My chief care," he writes there, " in choosing my lodging is always to avoid a thick and stinking air; and those beautiful cities, Venice and Paris, very much lessen the kindness I have for them, the one by the offensive smell of her marshes and the other of that of her dirt." We do not even get an impression as vivid as that from his account of his visit.

Montaigne came to Venice from Fusina, as Boccaccio had done before him. It was the common entry. He dined there, and tells us the place was merely an inn where people embarked for Venice. " There," he says, " all the boats coming down the river are landed by means of a machine worked by two horses, in much the same way as they turn oil mills; and the boats are then carried on wheels to a place where they are launched on the canal which runs to the sea, near the point where Venice stands.

" After dinner we hired a gondola and proceeded five miles to Venice." It was, thus, on an evening at the end of October that Montaigne entered

64

"THE REDENTORE"

Venice. " Next day, which was Sunday, in the morning M. de Montaigne went to call on M. de Ferrier, the ambassador, who received him with open arms, accompanied him to Mass, and kept him to dinner." He does not tell us in which church they heard Mass, but in a side note he declares that Ferrier was a pedant, and inclined towards the innovations of Calvin. All the same we find Montaigne dining with him again on Monday in the company of another Frenchman. Ferrier then told him that he held no sort of correspondence with the Venetians, or indeed any man in the city, for, said he, " the authorities here are so suspicious that if any of their people were to speak but twice with me I should be immediately regarded with distrust." This, Montaigne tells us, very much influenced him. He immediately adds, no doubt with a fine irony, but to our endless disappointment : " The curiosities of this place are so well known that I need say nothing about them." He adds rather cryptically that he found Venice different from what he had imagined it to be, and was, indeed, somewhat disappointed after he had visited the various parts of it, which he did with great attention. The system of government, the situation of the place, the arsenal, the Piazza of S. Mark, and the concourse of foreigners seemed to him the most remarkable features.

When he had been there a week he notes that while he was at supper he received a small volume of letters she had written from Signora Veronica Franca, an Italian lady. Whether as a result of reading this small volume or of the smell from the marshes, on the following day he tells us he had a fit of the colic which lasted two or three hours. . . .

As to the Venetian women, famous through all Europe for their beauty, he tells us that he did not think them so handsome by any means as he had heard they were, and yet he says he saw " several of those ladies who make a traffic of their beauty." He was " exceedingly struck, as much so as with anything else, with the style in which some hundred and fifty or so of the principal courtesans live ; their houses are kept up, and themselves maintained and dressed quite as magnificently as though they were all princesses, and yet they have nothing to live upon but what they make by their profession. Some of them are kept by Venetian noblemen in the most open and public manner, there being no sort of attempt made to conceal the connection."

And that is all Montaigne has to say of Venice. He left on Saturday, November 12, early in the morning, after just a fortnight's stay in the city.

It is almost as disappointing to turn to the pages of another illustrious visitor who came to Venice a generation or more before Montaigne—Benvenuto Cellini. He has little more to recount than a row he and his friend Tribolo had with the sculptor Giacopo Sansovino. He came down the Po, and on his arrival he applied to a brother of Cardinal Cornaro for permission to wear his sword. He was told that he was at liberty to do so, and that the worst that could befall him was that he might lose it. Certainly if one may judge by the continual brawl he was in all the time he was in Venice, he was well advised.

It was on leaving Venice that, sleeping at a place near Chioggia, he had his famous quarrel with the inn-keeper, who insisted on being paid overnight. " I replied that when people insist on having things their own way they should make a world of their own ; but the practice of this State of ours was very different. The landlord said, ' That it did not signify disputing the matter, for he was determined it should be so.'

66

Tribolo trembled with fear, and by signs entreated me to be quiet lest the man should do something worse ; so we paid him in the manner he required, and went to bed. We had very fine new beds, with everything else new, and in the utmost elegance. Notwithstanding all this, I never closed my eyes the whole night, being entirely engaged in meditating revenge for the insolent treatment of our landlord. Now it came into my head to set the house on fire, and now to kill four good horses which the fellow had in his stable. I thought it was no difficult matter to put either design in execution, but did not see how I could easily secure my own escape and that of my fellow-traveller afterwards. At last I resolved to put my luggage into the ferry, and requesting my companions to go on board, I fastened the horses to the rope that drew the vessel, desiring my friends not to move it till my return, because I had left a pair of slippers in the room where I lay. This being settled, I went back to the inn, and enquired for the landlord, who told me that he had nothing to say to me, and that we might all go to the devil. There happened to be a little stable-boy in the inn who appeared quite drowsy. He told me that his master would not stir a foot for the Pope himself, and asked me to give him something to drink my health ; so I gave him some small Venetian coin, and desired him to stay outside with the ferryman till I had searched for my slippers. I went upstairs, carrying with me a little knife, which had an exceedingly sharp edge, and with it I cut four beds till I had done damage to the value of upwards of fifty crowns. I then returned to the ferry with some scraps of bedclothes in my pocket, and ordered the person who held the cable to which the ferry was tied, to set off with all speed. When we were got to some little distance from the inn, my friend Tribolo said 'that he had left behind him some

67

little leather straps with which he used to tie his cloak bag and that he wanted to go back in search of them.' I desired him not to trouble his head about two little straps of leather, and assured him that I would make him as many large ones as he should have occasion for. He told me that I was very merry, but that he was resolved to return for his leather straps ; but as he called out to the ferryman to stop, I bid him go on, and in the meantime told Tribolo all the damage I had done at the inn, in proof of which I produced some of the scraps of the bedclothes. He thereupon was seized with a panic so violent that he never ceased crying out to the ferryman to make haste, and did not think himself secure from danger till we arrived at the gates of Florence."

But it is not in truth in the ideal poetry of Shakespeare, or the intellectual egoism and irony of Montaigne, or even in the naive malice of Cellini that we really get a picture of the Venice of the sixteenth century. Something evil and corrupt had entered into the civilization of all Europe at this time, and not least of Italy. The Middle Age which had held out to humanity so great a promise had in some inexplicable way and for some inexplicable reason failed, failed in endurance and in life. The fifteenth century had been full of disaster almost everywhere save only in Venice, and even Venice could not escape the spiritual disaster which that century made apparent. For with the sixteenth century we are face to face with the spiritual break-up of Europe and European society. Something evil, depraved, venal and mean appears. The pen is bought and sold, futile praise and blame are purchased by popes, kings, prelates, and we see an infamous scoundrel of genius wander across Europe blackmailing, and blackmailing successfully, every authority, every power. That scoundrel was Aretino, and he was at home in Venice, and in Venice

68

"PALAZZO DEI CAMERLENGHI"

passed no inconsiderable portion of his days. For the Venice of the sixteenth century was a promised land for such as he. A city of wealthy merchants, an aristocratic oligarchy fast degenerating into plutocracy, in which snobs abounded, as well as scholars, Venice was then the greatest independent metropolis in Europe, insolent and artistic, the great asylum for exiles, for the proscribed, the chance poor scholar, the perverted and the corrupt. For she could offer to all of them alike this great gift— liberty. And it is in the letters of the very type and paragon of all these together that we find perhaps the best picture of the city at this time—in the letters of Aretino, who, vile as he was, was yet a man of genius ; scoundrel though he was, was yet full of humanity ; brutal though he was, was yet full of pity and love for the miserable, the unfortunate, the poor ; ignoble though he was, was yet able to dominate the Italy of his time : whom Francis I honoured, Charles V spoke with familiarly and Ariosto surnamed *il divino*. Here in Venice he was the friend of Titian, the correspondent of Michaelangelo. Here in Venice he lived like a prince though he had nothing solid under his feet, he was as insolent as a *condottiere*, though he had rendered no service, he was the most famous man in the city, though his record was merely infamous. An epoch had appeared which was an anarchy, in which everything was questioned, everything doubtful ; in which anything might happen and anything might be thought to be true, an epoch without principles and without authority ; in which a charlatan of genius might do anything, might destroy the unity of Europe or the spiritual and philosophical basis upon which Europe stood, by one multiple weapon—calumny.

But let us first of all try to get a picture of the Venice of this time in its outward appearance. That can of course best be obtained from

69

the pictures of the time, but we have a description left us by a son of Venice, boastful and insolent, it is true, which I take from that very curious book *Delle cose Notabili della Città di Venezia*, by Francesco Sansovino, published in Venice in 1561.

"There is not," he boasts, "a town in all Europe which has more or larger palaces than this town of Venice; but we call them houses, not palaces, out of modesty, giving the name of *palazzo* only to that of the Doge. And yet, though you go through all the principal towns of Italy—Rome, Naples, Milan, Genoa, Florence, Bologna, etc.—you will not find one which can show you more than three or four dwellings truly meriting the name of Palace, while in Venice you may count them by hundreds. Outside the town, towards the mainland, there are some houses, it is true, built in the earlier time of the republic which make a poor show and bear witness to the meanness of the ancient owners. They are low and their windows narrow. . . . Our old writers tell us that in the old days our ancestors wished to show their unity and equality in all things, and built their houses all of the same height. But commerce has enriched us, and so they came to be built high or low according to the will of their owners. Almost all our palaces are built in the finest situations and at the most beautiful points of view in the town. The greater number stand on the water, and before them have a quay. Each, too, has its *terrazza* on the roof, made of wood or stone. These terraces are called *altane*. All are covered in with flat roofs of tiles, the water being carried off in gutters into cisterns. Every piazza and every courtyard has its public fountain. Under Doge Foscari alone the Government built more than thirty for the use of the poor. The foundations of the buildings are established by means of very strong piles of oak which harden

70

in the water. These piles are driven into their bed and are supported by transverse piles of great size, the intervals being filled with cement and fragments of rock, these forming a very firm foundation for any sort of work or building however heavy. Add to all this that all our windows are closed, not as elsewhere with waxed linen or paper, but with very clear and strong glass secured by iron and lead, and these glass windows are not a luxury of the palaces and noble houses but are universally to be found to the astonishment of foreigners. Well, all these good things come from our furnaces of Murano. As for the furniture, I have seen the old customary furniture of our patricians sold which would have been much too fine to look for in the most sumptuous palaces of the grand dukes of Italy."[1]

[1] F. Sansovino : *Delle cose Notabili della Città di Venezia.* Bk. 9.

71

## VIII

## ARETINO IN VENICE.

INTO this city it was that Aretino came in the spring of 1527. He came there almost as a refugee at the age of thirty-five. Known only for his scurrilous libels, having been expelled from Rome and other cities, he came to Venice really to consider the situation ; and the licence, the luxury, the splendour and the liberty of the place pleasing him, he came little by little to settle down there. He at once made friends with the Doge, Andrea Gritti, writing him the most adulatory letter, and asked for and obtained his protection. " Here am I," he writes to the Doge, " who in the liberty of this great State have learned already to be free, and I renounce for ever the court of Rome, and I intend to establish in this place my eternal habitation." Well, Aretino had decided wisely : there was no city so suitable for his purpose as Venice. He lived by libel, and he needed the Press. In this city of printers and the Press, in its liberty and licence, he found exactly what he wanted.

He had been *en rapport* with Jacopo Sansovino the sculptor. This man

72

became the fast friend of Aretino and rendered him one supreme service : he introduced him to Titian. It was thus was founded a triumvirate— Titian, Aretino, Sansovino—which presently became famous. All this happened very quickly. Aretino had not been three months in Venice when we find him writing to the Marchese Gonzaga with regard to his portrait by Titian.

We may perhaps ask what can have been the attraction of such a man as Aretino for the noble Titian. This certainly, that Aretino, who respected nothing, respected the arts. But to ask such a question is to misunderstand not only Aretino but still more Titian himself. A thousand things bound them together : interest, for the great journalist of the age could multiply fame as easily as infamy ; then life, for Aretino was undoubtedly one of the most living and the most rich personalities of his day ; he could give Titian as much as he took from him. All Italy was known to Aretino ; he had been indulged at every Court ; he knew everything about everybody ; he enjoyed enormously everything about everybody. His intellect, too, was of the highest order ; he understood everything and perhaps everybody. In a sense he must have completed Titian. That Tuscan mind, for Aretino was of Arezzo, was like a sword, and in Venice like a sword where all the rest were less highly tempered. His excesses had not dulled his wit or made his irony less biting, less enchanting. He must not only have completed but have amused Titian. Titian painted him, and he certainly never had a more splendid or a richer subject. He painted him over and over again : first in the portrait now in the Pitti Palace, then in that in the Chigi Palace at Rome. He appears too as Pilate in the *Ecco Homo* now in Vienna. They enjoyed life together intellectually, socially and sensually. Aretino is true in his friendship.

L

Indefatigably he advertises Titian, writes innumerable letters about him and his pictures to Francis I, to Charles V, to Ottaviano de' Medici, to everyone; writes sonnets on Titian's works and talks, talks, talks to everyone about his friend. His letters are indeed the principal source of information on Titian's life for about thirty years.

As for Aretino: "Titian is to me another I," he writes, and again, "he is I and I am he," and again, "when I write to you it is the same as if the letters were from Titian," and Marcolini, who knew them both intimately, writes to Aretino, "Titian is to you more than a brother." They were not only constantly together, they shared everything. If Aretino received from one of his numerous patrons, or more numerous victims, some delicacy for the table, he writes at once to Titian to come and share it with him, and invites Sansovino and some fair and fragile lady to join them. If Aretino, whose house was like an inn, felt the number of his guests too many, he fled to Titian. That his house was like a public inn we know from himself: "So many gentlemen break in on me continually with visits that my stairs are worn with their feet like the pavement of the Capitol with the wheels of triumphal cars. I do not believe that Rome itself has ever seen so great a mixture of nationalities as you may see in my house. To me come Turks, Jews, Indians, Frenchmen, Germans, Spaniards. You may gather how many Italians I have." No wonder he fled to Titian.

We get a glimpse of the triumvirate at dinner in Titian's house in a letter of the time:

"I was invited in the month of August to the house of Messer Tiziano Vecelli, a great painter as every one knows, and the most charming of hosts, to celebrate the festa known here as *ferrare agosto*. We were

74

assembled in a delicious garden situated at one extremity of Venice, beside the lagoon, across which rises the little island of Murano. In waiting for the table to be laid under the trees when the heat of the day should be over, we visited the house of the painter, full of the most marvellous pictures in the world. Then in the coolness of evening we saw the whole lagoon cover itself with gondolas carrying musicians and singers, who, together with the loveliest Venetian girls, began a serenade which lasted till midnight. As for the dinner it was as delicate as it was well ordered : the wines were fine and the accompanying service lacked nothing. At dessert they brought me your letter in which you praise the Latin tongue to the detriment of the Tuscan. Aretino attacked your opinion in the most brilliant and delightful fashion, and I should like to have in ink on paper his discourse. All passed in delight and gallantry. The noble and grave Titian kept all the time a certain restraint ; whilst Aretino's friends allowed themselves to be enticed by the charms of the Aspasias of Venice, he contented himself with addressing them charmingly and caressing them ; but he only gave them the kiss of Socrates."

This long friendship with Titian is indeed the noble side of Aretino's life. His friendship was disinterested and pure. In such feasts as that set out above we ever see Titian as the grave observer. It is Aretino who, delighting not less than his friends in the beauty and society of women, excites their laughter, animates their passions, flatters and amuses them, just as he flattered and amused the greatest princes, asking in return their friendship, which indeed they gave him without reserve. We see at his own dinners all the most celebrated courtesans in the city, and there were conceived those *Raggionamenti* which have been the model of all the obscene works of the seventeenth and eighteenth centuries.

And his loves were innumerable : Paola, Laura, Angela Zaffeta, Contessa Madrina, Caterina Sandella, Angela Sara, Franceschina, Paulina Sirena, Marietta d'Oro, Pierina Riccia, and many others ! In fact he had in Venice a regular harem composed of all sorts of women who loved him, who depended upon him, and who as often as not without his protection would have been homeless. His generosity, his hospitality, his kindness to the unfortunate, were notorious, and he cared, too, for their children. The little daughter of Caterina Sandella received the name of Adria, for she was born in Venice and her father adored her without measure. He had medals struck in her honour, forced princes and dukes to contribute to her dot, and finally married her to a rich man in Urbino. He never legitimized any of them. " They are legitimate in my heart," he said.

He saw Angela Sara first as he passed under her window in a gondola and " was burnt by her beauty, splendidly lascivious, proud and passionate." He always compared her to the sun or the moon. She was a Venetian courtesan, as was Angela Zaffeta, whom he praised as the loveliest woman in Venice, and we often see her sitting between him and Titian at dinner with musicians and other painters. He seems to have had some sort of respect for her. " I give you the palm among all those who have lived your joyous life," he says. " License with you always wears a decent mask. Whoever spends his money on you is really persuaded that he is the gainer. How do you manage to make so many new friends without losing the old ? You distribute so well your glances and your smiles and your nocturnal rendezvous that no one complains, and quarrels and curses never come near you."

Perhaps the most amusing of these affairs was that he had with the wife of Giovanni Antonio Sirena, whose daughter he had held at the baptismal font. She was very pretty, wrote verses, and loved her husband, and Aretino wanted her platonic friendship. He wrote verses in her honour in which she appears as the siren, protesting all the time the high purity of his affection, the chastity of his intentions, and his veneration for her. But his ignoble life rendered this public homage dangerous for her. Her relations and her husband interfered, fearing she would be confounded with the crowd of his mistresses. So she was obliged to close her door on the poet and even to refuse to acknowledge him in passing. Then Aretino arose. He wrote to her husband a furious letter, a model of conceit and vanity. " My pen has made Madame Sirena immortal," he wrote. " Know you that Popes, kings and emperors think themselves happy when I desire to keep on good terms with them. Do you know that the Duke of Ferrara has sent me an ambassador with money because I would not go to pay him a visit ? Do you know that there is not a woman in the world who would not be proud to be chastely sung and celebrated in my verses ? A time will come when this very letter that I send you and that I deign to sign with my own hand will be a title of pride and nobility for your son."

But it was not always that he could bear himself in this manner. He was sometimes deceived and betrayed. Thus when Marietta d'Oro, one of the inhabitants of his harem, wished to go away he persuaded her to stay by promising to get her married. In fact he married her to his secretary, a young man of twenty years. Then to get rid of the young husband, Aretino sent him to Francis I to fetch him money that the king had promised him. Aretino accompanied him some of the way to make sure he would go, but when he returned he found that Marietta

77

had looted the house and had set sail for Cyprus. All Venice mocked him. Meanwhile the young husband, having obtained the money from Francis, on his way back had lost it all at play, in the presence of Cardinal Gaddi to Strozzi.

Aretino did not despair; he forced the Cardinal to make good the loss.

But these things meant nothing to Aretino. He could always defend himself against the world. Where he failed was to defend himself against himself. Perhaps the most extraordinary example of this is to be found in the story of his love for Pierina Riccia. She was quite a young girl, exquisite and fragile, with whom he fell in love on the eve of her marriage. He got rid of the *fidanzato* and took her to his home with the consent of her relations, even with the tacit consent of Monsignore Zicotto, her uncle. He loved and adored her : she filled his life, but he got nothing in return, and presently she fell ill of consumption. His devotion knew no bounds, he gave up everything to nurse her, and he nursed her most tenderly. The frightful malady made her almost repulsive, yet he tended her like a mother. She had to go to the hills ; he took her there, and during the whole of a winter made journey after journey across the bitter lagoon, the horrible roads, in wind and snow and rain, to spend a few hours with her. He was often frozen with cold and soaked with rain ; he made nothing of it. Then she began to get well under his marvellous care. He loaded her with gifts. She got quite well, and returning with him to Venice, left his home by stealth with a young lover.

Aretino was beside himself. After three years she returned. He still loved her and took her in. She gave him nothing. She fell ill again. He nursed her as before, but this time in vain. She died, and he never

78

got over this loss ; it colours the rest of his life, everything he does, all his thoughts and his work. " O famous doctor in philosophy," he writes to Barbaro, " if only you could teach me to forget."

But Aretino's house, like his life, contained other things besides the harem, the " Aretines."

This house stood, as I have said, on the Grand Canal half-way between the Ca d'Oro and the Rialto Bridge. Here he lived till in 1551 he went to the Riva del Carbin, where he died in 1557. That the house was thronged with every sort of visitor we have seen : that it was filled with women we know, but it was also full of all his loot, his rich habits and gowns with which he tells us not only Europe but Asia had furnished him. There, too, were his collections of pictures and curiosities. There were very few books. He had perhaps himself written too much humbug to care for them as a genuine man of letters would do. In the midst of the house was a noble *salone* under a glass dome. There were served his banquets, cooked by an admirable cook, governed by one of his women, Marietta. He never dined in the town, for according to him the Venetians knew neither how to eat nor how to drink. He kept open house and open table, and everyone from great lords to courtesans enjoyed his hospitality.

Another great *salone* was lined with ebony cabinets, in which he kept his letters ; there were separate compartments for those from princes, from cardinals, from captains, from great ladies, from musicians, from painters, from gentlemen and from merchants. Here Titian would often come to paint, for the room was very well lighted.

His own chamber was simple enough, and contained only a desk, some pens and paper. This was all he needed. He boasts of his independence of books. " I am a free man. I do not need to copy Petrarca or

79

Boccaccio. My own genius is enough. Let others worry themselves about style and so cease to be themselves. Without a master, without a model, without a guide, without artifice I go to work and win my living, my well-being and my fame. What do I need more? With a goose quill and a few sheets of paper I amuse myself with the universe. They say I am the son of a courtesan. It may be so; but I have the soul of a king. I live free, I enjoy myself, and I can call myself happy.

" You think you know all my glory, and you do not know half of it. Medals of me have been struck in gold, in silver, in lead, in copper, in bronze, and in terra-cotta. My effigy is placed on the façades of palaces. My head is engraved on combs, on plates, as the ornament of mirrors, like that of Alexander, or Cæsar or Scipio. Those vases they make at Murano are called after me. A breed of horses has been given my name, merely because I accepted one from Pope Clement VII. I sent it in my turn to Duke Federigo. The canal that washes one side of this house has been renamed Rio Aretino. My women like to be called Aretines : they even say *stilo Aretino*—the style of Aretino. I have nothing to envy anyone, nor can the breath of envy or the cloud of malice dim my renown or diminish the train of my house."

It is quite another Aretino who writes as follows to Titian : " Signore, my good gossip, despite my admirable habit, I dined alone to-day, or rather I dined in company with the quartan fever which serves me as an eternal escort and which does not allow me to taste any food I eat. You see me then rising from table filled with ennui and despair, having eaten almost nothing. I crossed my arms and I leaned over the window-sill, my head and shoulders outside, to look on the fair world there, my dear gossip.

80

"There I saw boats without number, loaded with strangers and natives, passing up and down the Grand Canal, the aspect of which always delights those who go upon it and seems in its turn to rejoice to bear a crowd of strangers. There were two gondolas tilting, and three were racing, and a crowd of people, watching the sport, filled the Rialto Bridge and overflowing on to the Riva and the Pescaria, filled the *traghetto* of S. Sophia and the steps of the Casa da Mosto. They applauded and shouted, and everyone going about his own affairs threw a glance at the race and clapped his hands. I, tormented and wearied with my fever, lifted my eyes to heaven.

"Indeed, since that day when God created the heavens, never have they been so fair, so full of light, so fair with clouds. It was a sky for the despair of painters, at least for all those that envy you, gossip mine! And the houses, the houses of stone, seemed like fairy palaces, here reflecting the pure clear light, there fading away into mist. Under the wandering shadows of the clouds, great white clouds charged with vapour, the buildings took on a thousand new beauties, they seemed no longer to be just buildings, but marvellous. To the right a palace was lost altogether in the deep shadow, it might have been built of ebony; to the left the marbles shone dazzling forth, as though the very sun had left the firmament and was imprisoned there. Before me the roofs shone with a bright vermilion. Nature, mistress of all masters! How miraculous is her brush, how wonderful her pencil! I know that your pencil, my Titian, is the rival of Nature, and you her most well beloved son: so I cried out three times, Titian, Titian, Titian, where art thou?"

In those few lines, written to please his friend, how wonderful a picture of Venice Aretino gives us! This man who lived on libel and

M

blackmail, and respected nothing but art, was himself an artist. He who had mercy on the poor, the wretched and the miserable, and only shewed his teeth to the rich, cannot have been wholly bad. His life was shameless, rowdy and disordered, so that Titian remonstrates with him and tells him his very servants mock him. Yet we learn they mocked him because " he treated them rather as his own daughters than as domestics." He laughed at Titian's advice, and likened himself to Philip, father of Alexander the Great, who in the midst of his triumphs demanded of the gods a little humiliation. As he says, he whom princes feared, what did he care though servants respected him not ? Yet I think he who was called the Scourge of Princes was often sad at heart.

Such a life as his, with his Aretines and his blackguard and hypocritical letters, his absolute freedom and his thronged house, thronged with the poor as well as with the famous, could only have been lived perhaps in Venice, and in a way it is a symbol of her decadence : outwardly, more glorious than ever before, but sick at heart. When at last he came to die, after having, as he said, refused a Cardinal's hat, he died like Venice was to die, covered with glory and shame. This befell Aretino in his sixty-sixth year at the end of 1557, and they buried him in the church of S. Luke, and in less than no time he was utterly forgotten.

## IX

## LEPANTO.

THAT the Venice in which Aretino's life was possible was a
very different Venice from that great Republic of the fourteenth and fifteenth centuries is evident. It could perhaps
only have been in a State which had passed its grand
climacteric that such a life could have been lived. That Venice was
already declining is certain. Her trade was going, and with her trade
her power. Already in 1535 it is a Venetian who can say, *Non si dà più
a negotiar in la città, ne alla navigation ne ad altra laudevole industria.*
Venice had ceased to accumulate and had begun to spend. Titian and
Tintoretto and Veronese might cover the walls of the great *salone* of the
Ducal Palace with beauty and glory and fame : it was poetry they dealt
in, emotion remembered in tranquillity. Both Titian and Tintoretto
knew the truth before they died, and expressed their anguish in those
tremendous canvasses that are still full of their despair. Veronese went
on dreaming through the marvellous courtyards and noble *saloni* where
Venice sat at meat amid a luxury of music and furniture unknown
elsewhere.

83

Venice was face to face with the decline; but so great and so noble a nation, by some fortune surely not undeserved, was to have one more glorious moment e'er she entered the shadow of the great evening. She was to fight and to win at Lepanto.

By the middle of the sixteenth century, Venice had lost all her possessions in the East to the Turks, except a few Dalmatian coast towns and certain islands, the greater of which were Corfù, Crete and Cyprus. Indeed, it was only her great naval power that still saved these to her. The Turks knew nothing of the sea, and when Corfù had been attacked the Turks had relied on their pirate ally Barbarossa. But by 1570 the Porte was very formidable at sea, in fact the greatest sea power in the world. This had been achieved by a reckless use of men and money, both of which the Turks had in abundance. They could always replace both men and ships when they were lost, and they could hire any number of mercenary sailors. The Turkish fleet on the eve of Lepanto boasted not less than three hundred sail in being.

To face this enormous armament Venice might with difficulty man a hundred ships. But she had the sea in her blood, a glorious reputation on the waters, and both wit and courage. Peace with the Turks had endured for a generation when a new Sultan, Selim, ascended the throne in Constantinople. He coveted Cyprus, not only for that it was a fine naval station, but for its wines and fertility. It seemed to him also that it would be easy to take, since it was so far from Venice. He knew the garrison was weak, and he believed that the arsenal had been destroyed by an explosion. He therefore sent to demand its surrender. "You must surrender it freely, or I will take it," said he. "Beware how you

84

provoke me, for my terrible sword will find you out everywhere, and as for your treasure it shall run from you like water."

At this insolence Venice arose. Yet she knew the garrison and defences at Cyprus were weak and the Cypriotes not too well affected : she knew that she dare not face the Turkish fleet alone, though she did not know it to be as formidable as it was. She turned to find allies : the Pope, Spain, Genoa.

Meanwhile the Turks fell upon Cyprus, which was heroically defended by Marcantonio Bragadin. All the Venetian women on the island were carried off as slaves for the harems of the East. One of them—we do not know her name—blew up the ship that bore them away and thus saved herself and her companions from something worse than death. Bragadin was defeated and taken. They cut off his nose and his ears, and obliged him to witness the barbarous death of his comrades Tiepolo, Martinengo, Baglione and Quirini, whom they stoned, hanged and hacked to death before his eyes, and ruthlessly murdered a vast number of men, women and children. When his turn came, they hung him up by the hands in the midst of the town, and there slowly, slowly, slowly, skinned him alive. Then they stuffed his skin and carried it about the streets and made sport, and tying it to the masthead of their flagship they bore it away to Constantinople. But one who loved him risked his life and went into the great city and with almost superhuman cunning stole the terrible thing away and brought it to Venice where it is preserved in the church of SS. Giovanni e Paolo.

Then came young Don John of Austria ; twenty-six years old he was, and Venice having found her allies led the great fleets which represented Christendom into battle. They found the Beast at Lepanto and fell upon

85

him without ado. And they left his crooked ships at the bottom of our sea, and they slew the accursed Turk to the number of 80,000. Would that the Crescent had perished there for ever. Oh, had old blind Dandolo but had that fleet! Then had Christendom been driven on to Constantinople and the Turk, the assassin of the East, had been destroyed altogether or driven for ever into that dark Asia whence he came. Alas, it was not to be. So great, so noble, so splendid a Crusade was as far beyond their energy as ours.

All this befell on an October day in the year 1571. On the eighteenth of that month a great galley of war, which bore the name of *Gabriel Archangel*, for it came to make annunciation, sailed into Venice, bright with flags, and drawing behind her the loot of the Beast, Crescents, turbans, Turkish coats and standards. And the cannon of the arsenal answered hers, and over Venice once again victory spread her wings, and the great bell of S. Mark rang out, and all the bells of all the *Sestieri* and of all islands through all the lagoons gave answer and Venice resounded like a city of bronze. But though all the city was mad with joy, not a single Turk in his Quarter was killed : instead, with Doge Mocenigo at their head, Venice went into S. Marco to sing Te Deum.

Let them sing, while they drape the city in scarlet, and shew their treasures to the sun, and pile up the Turkish arms in Piazza S. Marco and hang their Titians and their Tintorettos in the Rialto : they got no more than joy out of that victory. In a single year the Beast was up and out again. "Lepanto," as was said, "might as well have been a Turkish victory."

Just as Lepanto for all its rumour and its success only throws a brilliant ray of light upon the decay of the Venetian State, so the strange

"PALAZZO LISATI"

episode of Paolo Sarpi, a man of genius and one of the greatest men of letters Venice ever produced, is only an episode, and serves but to light up the decay of the city.

Venice had, in part at least owing to her geographical position, always maintained a somewhat independent attitude towards the Vatican. We see it in the law which established that every Patriarch of Venice must be a Venetian, while the Holy Office was unable to act there except by the consent of the Venetian Government. Even in the fourteenth century we find the Doge declaring that the Pope has nothing to do with temporal affairs, and the Press too, from its inception, was freer in Venice than perhaps anywhere else in Europe. Venice, however, had always desired to live on good terms with the Papacy, and this more than ever after the League of Cambray (1508). Towards the end of the sixteenth century, however, there were several difficult questions pending between the Pope and Venice, and these were not rendered less difficult by the general upheaval of the Reformation and the loss to the Church of the whole of Northern Europe. Indeed these questions, not crucial in themselves, perhaps, came soon to appear crucial for political reasons, and it presently became a question whether Venice would abandon what she regarded as her immemorial rights and privileges conceded by former Popes, or whether she would face an Interdict. In fact she was given twenty-four days to make up her mind.

Now in all this quarrel the man whose mind inspired the action of the Republic was Fra Paolo Sarpi, a Servite, born at Venice in 1552. The Interdict was launched, the Papal Nuncio was given his passports, Venice was excommunicated. The Jesuits with the Capuchins and the Theatines sided with the Pope and were expelled the city. There followed a mighty

87

war of pamphlets while Europe looked on. But, in spite of the genius of Sarpi, Venice was in an impossible position because she was not Protestant; she was Catholic, though her sons were wont to say " We are Venetians first and then Christians." England, Holland and the German Powers were no good to her: her philosophy was not theirs. But as it happened the moment was past. The prestige of Spain, whose power she most feared, was broken in 1588 with the defeat of the Armada, and the Pope, having more than enough on his hands, was ready to admit the good offices of France. Venice was ready to compromise, and relations were resumed between Rome and Venice. Sarpi, who had supported the whole weight of the controversy on behalf of the Republic, was stabbed almost to death outside his convent, but fortunately he recovered and lived to an honoured old age in Venice. He seems to have been but another victim of that enormous controversy which wrecked all Europe— the dispute concerning the supremacy of the State, which politically was the very kernel of the Reformation.

88

## X

## VENICE IN THE SEVENTEENTH CENTURY.

THUS in a gathering darkness Venice passed out of the sixteenth into the seventeenth century.

Of the spectacle she offered in the first half of the *seicento* we have fortunately a quite elaborate record from an English pen—that of John Evelyn.

John Evelyn left England in 1641 really to avoid the troubles of the Civil War. He had set out to join the King at Brentford, but when the result of that battle was known, he hesitated because, as he said, his own estates and those of his brother were so near to London as to be in the full power of the Parliament, and that consequently if he joined the King he would be certainly ruined without any gain to His Majesty. So he obtained the King's permission to travel and set out for Flushing on July 21st. He came to Venice in June, 1645, after having seen Holland, Flanders, France and the greater part of Italy, including Rome, Naples and Florence. In the Diary that records his travels he gives us one of the best pictures of Venice to be had of that or any other time.

N

He came to Venice from Ferrara by the Po and the Adige and so by sea to Chioggia, landing at Malamocco " about seven at night, after we had stayed at least two hours for permission to land, our bill of health being delivered according to custom. As soon as we came on shore we were conducted to the Dogana, where our portmanteaux were visited and then we got to our lodging, which was at honest Signor Paulo Rhodomante's, at the *Black Eagle*, near the Rialto, one of the best quarters of the town."

Being very weary and beaten with the journey Evelyn went to one of the baths where he was treated " after the Eastern manner, washing with hot and cold water, with oils, and being rubbed with a kind of strigel of seal's skin, put on the operator's hand like a glove." This bath so opened his pores that he caught " one of the greatest colds I ever had in my life " ; but this does not seem to have prevented him from at once going to see the sights. He found Venice " the most wonderfully placed of any city in the world, built on so many hundred islands in the very sea, and at good distance from the Continent."

He was in time to see the Doge wed the sea on Ascension Day, and all that vast procession and festa. " The Doge," he says, " having heard Mass in his robes of state (which are very particular, after the Eastern fashion) together with the Senate in their gowns, embarked in their gloriously painted, carved and gilded Bucintoro, environed and followed by innumerable galleys, gondolas, and boats, filled with spectators, some dressed in masquerade, trumpets, music and cannons."

He then gives us the following description of the gondola. " Two days after, taking a gondola, which is their water coach, we rode up and down the channels which answer to our streets. These vessels are built very long and narrow, having necks and tails of steel, somewhat spreading at the beak like a fishes tail and kept so exceedingly polished as to give a great lustre; some are adorned with carving, others lined with velvet, (commonly black), with curtains and tassels, and the seats like couches, to lie stretched on, while he who rows stands upright on the very edge of the boat, and, with one oar, bending forward as if he would fall into the sea, rows and turns with incredible dexterity; thus passing from channel to channel, landing his fare or patron at what house he pleases. The beaks of these vessels are not unlike the ancient Roman rostrums.

"The first public building I went to see was the Rialto, a bridge of one arch over the grand canal, so large as to admit a galley to row under it, built of good marble, and having on it, besides many pretty shops, three ample and stately passages for people without any inconvenience, the two outmost nobly balustred with the same stone; a piece of architecture much to be admired. It was evening, and the canal where the Noblesse go to take the air, as in our Hyde-park, was full of ladies and gentlemen. There are many times dangerous stops, by reason of the multitude of gondolas ready to sink one another; and indeed they affect to lean them on one side, that one who is not accustomed to it, would be afraid of oversetting. Here they were singing, playing on harpsichords and other music, and serenading their mistresses; in another place, racing, and other pastimes on the water, it being now exceeding hot.

"Next day, I went to their Exchange, a place like ours, frequented by merchants, but nothing so magnificent: from thence my guide led me to the Fondaco dei Tedeschi, which is their magazine, and here many of the merchants, especially Germans, have their lodging and diet, as in a

91

college. The outside of this stately fabric is painted by Giorgione da Castelfranco, and Titian himself.

" Hence I passed through the Merceria, one of the most delicious streets in the world for the sweetness of it, and is all the way on both sides tapestried as it were with cloth of gold, rich damasks and other silks, which the shops expose and hang before their houses from the first floor, and with that variety that for near half the year spent chiefly in this city, I hardly remember to have seen the same piece twice exposed ; to this add the perfumes, apothecaries' shops, and the innumerable cages of nightingales, which they keep, that entertain you with their melody from shop to shop, so that shutting your eyes, you would imagine yourself in the country, when indeed you are in the middle of the sea. It is almost as silent as the middle of a field, there being neither rattling of coaches nor trampling of horses. This street, paved with brick, and exceedingly clean, brought us through an arch into the famous piazza of S. Mark.

" Over this porch stands that admirable clock, celebrated next to that of Strasburg for its many movements ; amongst which, about twelve and six, which are their hours of Ave Maria, when all the town are on their knees, come forth the three Kings led by a star, and passing by the image of Christ in his Mother's arms, do their reverence, and enter into the clock by another door. At the top of this turret another automaton strikes the quarters. An honest merchant told me that one day walking in the piazza, he saw the fellow who kept the clock struck with this hammer so forcibly, as he was stooping his head near the bell, to mend something amiss at the instant of striking, that being stunned, he reeled over the battlements, and broke his neck. The buildings in this piazza are all

arched, on pillars, paved within with black and white polished marble, even to the shops, the rest of the fabric as stately as any in Europe, being not only marble, but the architecture is of the famous Sansovino, who lies buried in S. Giacomo at the end of the piazza. The battlements of this noble range of building are railed with stone, and thick-set with excellent statues, which add a great ornament. One of the sides is yet much more Roman-like than the other which regards the sea, and where the church is placed. The other range is plainly Gothic: and so we entered into S. Mark's Church, before which stand two brass pedestals exquisitely cast and figured which bear as many tall masts painted red, on which, upon great festivals, they hang flags and streamers. The church is also Gothic; yet for the preciousness of the materials, being of several rich marbles, abundance of porphyry, serpentine, etc., far exceeding any in Rome, S. Peter's hardly excepted. I much admired the splendid history of our blessed Saviour, composed all of mosaic over the *facciata*, below which and over the chief gates are cast four horses in copper as big as the life, the same that formerly were transported from Rome by Constantine to Byzantium and thence by the Venetians hither. They are supported by eight porphyry columns, of very great size and value. Being come into the church, you see nothing, and tread on nothing, but what is precious. The floor is all inlaid with agates, lazulis, chalcedons, jaspers, porphyries, and other rich marbles, admirable also for the work; the walls sumptuously incrusted, and presenting to the imagination the shapes of men, birds, houses, flowers, and a thousand varieties. The roof is of most excellent mosaic; but what most persons admire is the new work of the emblematic tree at the other passage out of the church. In the midst of this rich *volto* rise five cupolas, the middle very large and

93

sustained by thirty-six marble columns, eight of which are of precious marbles : under these cupolas is the high altar, on which is a reliquary of several sorts of jewels, engraven with figures, after the Greek manner, and set together with plates of pure gold. The altar is covered with a canopy of ophite, on which is sculptured the story of the Bible, and so on the pillars, which are of Parian marble, that support it. Behind these are four other columns of transparent and true oriental alabaster, brought hither out of the mines of Solomon's Temple, as they report. There are many chapels and notable monuments of illustrious persons, dukes, cardinals, etc., as Zeno, J. Soranzi and others ; there is likewise a vast baptistery, of copper. Among other venerable relics is a stone, on which they say our Blessed Lord stood preaching to those of Tyre and Sidon, and the door is an image of Christ, much adorned, esteeming it very sacred, for that a rude fellow striking it, they say, there gushed out a torrent of blood. In one of the corners lies the body of S. Isidore, brought hither five hundred years since from the island of Chios. A little farther they shew the picture of S. Dominic and S. Francis, affirmed to have been made by the Abbot Joachim (many years before any of them were born). Going out of the church, they shewed us the stone where Alexander III trod on the neck of the Emperor Frederick Barbarossa, pronouncing that verse of the Psalm, ' super basiliscum,' etc. The doors of the church are of massy copper. There are near five hundred pillars in this building, most of them porphyry and ser-pentine, and brought chiefly from Athens, and other parts of Greece, formerly in their power. At the corner of the church, are inserted into the main wall four figures, as big as life, cut in porphyry ; which they say are the images of four brothers who poisoned one another, by which means were escheated to the Republic that vast treasury of relics now belonging to the church. At the other entrance that looks towards the sea, stands in a small chapel that statue of our Lady, made (as they affirm) of the same stone, or rock, out of which Moses brought water to the murmuring Israelites at Horeb or Meriba.

" After all that is said, this church is, in my opinion, much too dark and dismal, and of heavy work ; the fabric—as is much of Venice, both for buildings and other fashions and circumstances,—after the Greeks, their next neighbours.

" The next day, by favour of the French ambassador, I had admittance with him to view the Reliquary, called here Tesoro di San Marco, which very few, even of travellers, are admitted to see. It is a large chamber full of presses. There are twelve breastplates or pieces of pure golden armour, studded with precious stones, and as many crowns dedicated to S. Mark by so many noble Venetians, who had recovered their wives taken at sea by the Saracens ; many curious vases of agates ; the cap, or coronet, of the Dukes of Venice, one of which had a ruby set on it esteemed worth 200,000 crowns ; two unicorns' horns ; numerous vases and dishes of agate, set thick with precious stones and vast pearls ; divers heads of Saints, enchased in gold ; a small ampulla, or glass, with our Saviour's blood ; a great morsel of the real Cross ; one of the nails ; a thorn ; a fragment of the column to which our Lord was bound when scourged ; the standard, or ensign, of Constantine ; a piece of S. Luke's arm ; a rib of S. Stephen ; a finger of Mary Magdalen ; numerous other things, which I could not remember. But a priest, first vesting himself in his sacerdotals, with the stole about his neck, showed us the gospel of S. Mark (their tutelar patron) written by his own hand, and whose body

95

they shew buried in the church, brought hither from Alexandria many years ago.

"A French gentleman and myself went to the Courts of Justice, the Senate-house, and Ducal Palace. The first court near this church is almost wholly built of several coloured sorts of marble, like chequer-work on the outside; this is sustained by vast pillars, not very shapely, but observable for their capitals, and that out of thirty-three no two are alike. Under this fabric is the cloister where merchants meet morning and evening, as also the grave senators and gentlemen, to confer of state affairs, in their gowns and caps, like so many philosophers; it is a very noble and solemn spectacle. In another quadrangle, stood two square columns of white marble, carved, which they said had been erected to hang one of their Dukes on, who designed to make himself Sovereign. Going through a stately arch, there were standing in niches divers statues of great value, amongst which is the so celebrated Eve, esteemed worth its weight in gold; it is just opposite to the stairs where are two Colossuses of Mars and Neptune, by Sansovino. We went up into a Corridor built with several Tribunals and Courts of Justice; and by a well-contrived staircase were landed in the Senate-hall, which appears to be one of the most noble and spacious rooms in Europe, being seventy-six paces long, and thirty-two in breadth. At the upper end, are the Tribunals of the Doge, Council of Ten, and Assistants: in the body of the hall, are lower ranks of seats, capable of containing one thousand five hundred Senators; for they consist of no fewer on grand debates. Over the Duke's throne are the paintings of the 'Final Judgment' by Tintoret, esteemed among the best pieces in Europe. On the roof are the famous Acts of the Republic, painted by several excellent masters, especially Bassano; next them, are the effigies of the several Dukes, with their Elogies. Then, we turned into a great Court painted with the Battle of Lepanto, an excellent piece; afterwards, into the Chamber of the Council of Ten, painted by the most celebrated masters. From hence, by the special favour of an Illustrissimo, we were carried to see the private Armoury of the Palace, and so to the same court we first entered, nobly built of polished white marble, part of which is the Duke's Court, *pro tempore;* there are two wells adorned with excellent work, in copper. This led us to the sea-side, where stand those columns of ophite stone in the entire piece, of a great height, one bearing S. Mark's Lion, the other S. Theodorus; these pillars were brought from Greece, and set up by Nicholas Baraterius, the architect; between them public executions are performed.

"Having fed our eyes with the noble prospect of the Island of S. George, the galleys, gondolas, and other vessels passing to and fro, we walked under the cloister on the other side of this goodly piazza, being a most magnificent building, the design of Sansovino. Here we went into the *Zecca*, or Mint: at the entrance stand two prodigious giants, or Hercules, of white marble; we saw them melt, beat, and coin silver, gold, and copper. We then went up into the Procuratory, and a library of excellent MSS. and books belonging to it and the public. After this we climbed up the tower of S. Mark, which we might have done on horseback, as it is said one of the French Kings did; there being no stairs or steps, but returns that take up an entire square on the arches forty feet, broad enough for a coach. This steeple stands by itself, without any church near it, and is rather a watch tower in the corner of the great piazza, 230 feet in height, the foundation exceeding deep; on the top, is an angel, that turns with the wind; and from hence is a prospect down

o

the Adriatic, as far as Istria and the Dalmatian side, with the surprising sight of this miraculous city, lying in the bosom of the sea, in the shape of a lute, the numberless Islands tacked together by no fewer than four hundred and fifty bridges. At the foot of this tower, is a public tribunal of excellent work, in white marble polished, adorned with several brass statues, and figures of stone and mezzo-relievo, the performance of some rare artist.

" It was now Ascension-week, and the great mart, or fair, of the whole year was kept, every body at liberty and jolly; the noblemen stalking with their ladies on *choppines*. These are high-heeled shoes, particularly affected by these proud dames, or, as some say, invented to keep them at home, it being very difficult to walk with them; whence, one being asked how he liked the Venetian dames, replied, they were *mezzo carne, mezzo legno*, half flesh, half wood, and he would have none of them. The truth is, their garb is very odd, as seeming always in masquerade; their other habits also totally different from all nations. They wear very long crisp hair, of several streaks and colours, which they make so by a wash, dishevelling it on the brims of a broad hat that has no crown, but a hole to put out their heads by; they dry them in the sun, as one may see them at their windows. In their tire, they set silk flowers and sparkling stones, their petticoats coming from their very armpits, so that they are near three quarters and a half apron; their sleeves are made exceeding wide, under which their shift-sleeves as wide, and commonly tucked up to the shoulder, showing their naked arms, through false sleeves of tiffany, girt with a bracelet or two, with knots of point richly tagged about their shoulders and other places of their body, which they usually cover with a kind of yellow veil of lawn, very transparent. Thus attired, they set

98

"PALAZZO"

their hands on the heads of two matron-like servants, or old women, to support them, who are mumbling their beads. It is ridiculous to see how these ladies crawl in and out of their gondolas, by reason of their *choppines;* and what dwarfs they appear, when taken down from their wooden scaffolds; of these I saw near thirty together, stalking half as high again as the rest of the world. For courtezans, or the citizens, may not wear *choppines,* but cover their bodies and faces with a veil of a certain glittering taffeta, or lustree, out of which they now and then dart a glance of their eye, the whole face being otherwise entirely hid with it; nor may the common misses take this habit; but go abroad bare-faced. To the corner of these virgin veils hang broad but flat tassels of curious Point de Venice. The married women go in black veils. The nobility wear the same colour, but a fine cloth lined with taffeta, in summer, with fur of the bellies of squirrels, in the winter, which all put on at a certain day, girt with a girdle embossed with silver; the vest not much different from what our Bachelors of Arts wear in Oxford, and a hood of cloth, made like a sack, cast over their left shoulder, and a round cloth black cap fringed with wool, which is not so comely; they also wear their collar open, to shew the diamond button of the stock of their shirt. I have never seen pearls for colour and bigness comparable to what the ladies wear, most of the noble families being very rich in jewels, especially pearls, which are always left to the son, or brother who is destined to marry; which the eldest seldom do. The Doge's vest is of crimson velvet, the Procurator's, etc., of damask, very stately. Nor was I less surprised with the strange variety of the several nations seen every day in the streets and piazzas; Jews, Turks, Armenians, Persians, Moors, Greeks, Sclavonians, some with their targets and bucklers, and all in their native fashions, negotiating in this famous Emporium, which is always crowded with strangers.

" This night, having with my Lord Bruce taken our places before, we went to the Opera, where comedies and other plays are represented in recitative music, by the most excellent musicians, vocal and instrumental, with variety of scenes painted and contrived with no less art of perspective, and machines for flying in the air, and other wonderful notions ; taken together, it is one of the most magnificent and expensive diversions the wit of man can invent. The history was, Hercules in Lydia ; the scenes changed thirteen times. The famous voices, Anna Rencia, a Roman, and reputed the best treble of women ; but there was an eunuch who, in my opinion, surpassed her ; also a Genoese that sung an incomparable bass. This held us by the eyes and ears till two in the morning, when we went to the Chetto di San Felice, to see the noblemen and their ladies at Basset, a game at cards which is much used ; but they play not in public, and all that have inclination to it are in masquerade, without speaking one word, and so they come in, play, lose or gain, and go away as they please. This time of licence is only in Carnival and this Ascension-Week ; neither are their theatres open for that other magnificence, or for ordinary comedians, save on these solemnities, they being a frugal and wise people, and exact observers of all sumptuary laws.

" The arsenal is thought to be one of the best furnished in the world. We entered by a strong port, always guarded, and, ascending a spacious gallery, saw arms of back, breast, and head, for many thousands ; in another were saddles ; over them ensigns taken from the Turks. Another hall is for the meeting of the Senate ; passing a graff are the smiths' forges, where they are continually employed on anchors and iron work.

Near it is a well of fresh water, which they impute to two rhinoceros's horns which they say lie in it, and will preserve it from ever being empoisoned. Then we came to where the carpenters were building their magazines of oars, masts, etc., for an hundred galleys and ships, which have all their apparel and furniture near them. Then the foundry, where they cast ordnance; the forge is four hundred and fifty paces long, and one of them has thirteen furnaces. There is one cannon, weighing 16,573 lbs., cast whilst Henry the Third dined, and put into a galley built, rigged, and fitted for launching within that time. They have also arms for twelve galeasses, which are vessels to row, of almost 150 feet long and thirty wide, not counting prow or poop, and contain twenty-eight banks of oars, each seven men, and to carry one thousand three hundred men, with three masts. In another, a magazine for fifty galleys, and place for some hundreds more. Here stands the Bucentaur, with a most ample deck, and so contrived that the slaves are not seen, having on the Poop a throne for the Doge to sit, when he goes in triumph to espouse the Adriatic. Here is also a gallery of 200 yards long for cables, and above that a magazine of hemp. Opposite these are the saltpetre houses, and a large row of cells, or houses, to protect their galleys from the weather. Over the gate, as we go out, is a room full of great and small guns, some of which discharge six times at once. Then there is a court full of cannon, bullets, chains, grapples, grenadoes, etc., and over that arms for eight hundred thousand men, and by themselves arms for four hundred, taken from some that were in a plot against the State; together with weapons of offence and defence for sixty-two ships; thirty-two pieces of ordnance, on carriages taken from the Turks, and one prodigious mortar-piece. In a word, it is not to be reckoned up what this large place contains of this sort. There were now twenty-three galleys and four galley-grossi, of one hundred oars of a side. The whole arsenal is walled about, and may be in compass about three miles, with twelve towers for the watch, besides that the sea environs it. The workmen, who are ordinarily five hundred, march out in military order, and every evening receive their pay through a small hole in the gate where the governor lives.

"The next day, I saw a wretch executed, who had murdered his master, for which he had his head chopped off by an axe that slid down a frame of timber, between the two tall columns in S. Mark's piazza, at the sea-brink; the executioner striking on the axe with a beetle; and so the head fell off the block.

"Hence, we went to see Grimani's Palace, the portico whereof is excellent work. Indeed, the world cannot shew a city of more stately buildings, considering the extent of it, all of square stone, and as charge-able in their foundations as superstructure, being all built on piles at an immense cost. We returned home by the church of S. Giovanni e Paolo, before which is, in copper, the statue of Bartolommeo Colleoni, on horseback, double gilt, on a stately pedestal, the work of Andrea Ver-rochio, a Florentine ! This is a very fine church, and has in it many rare altar-pieces of the best masters, especially that on the left hand, of the Two Friars slain, which is of Titian.

"The day after, being Sunday, I went over to S. George's to the ceremony of the schismatic Greeks, who are permitted to have their church, although they are at defiance with Rome. They allow no carved images, but many painted, especially the story of their patron and his dragon. Their rites differ not much from the Latins, save that of communicating in both species, and distribution of the holy bread. We

"A FESTA"

afterwards fell into a dispute with a Candiot, concerning the procession of the Holy Ghost. The church is a noble fabric.

"The church of S. Zachary is a Greek building, by Leo IV, Emperor, and has in it the bones of that prophet, with divers other saints. Near this, we visited S. Luke's, famous for the tomb of Aretino.

"Tuesday, we visited several other churches, as Santa Maria, newly incrusted with marble on the outside, and adorned with porphyry, ophite, and Spartan stone. Near the altar and under the organ, are sculptures, that are said to be of the famous artist, Praxiteles. To that of S. Paul I went purposely to see the tomb of Titian. Then to S. John the Evangelist, where, amongst other heroes, lies Andrea Baldarius, the inventor of oars applied to great vessels for fighting.

"We also saw S. Rocco, the roof whereof is, with the school, or hall, of that rich confraternity, admirably painted by Tintoretto, especially the Crucifix in the sacristy. We saw also the church of S. Sebastian, and Carmelites' monastery.

"Next day, taking our gondola at S. Mark's, I passed to the island of S. George *Maggiore*, where is a Convent of Benedictines and a well-built church of Andrea Palladio, the great architect. The pavement, cupola, choir, and pictures, very rich and sumptuous. The cloister has a fine garden to it, which is a rare thing at Venice, though this is an island a little distant from the city; it has also an olive orchard, all environed by the sea. The new cloister now building has a noble staircase paved with white and black marble.

"From hence, we visited Santo Spirito and S. Laurence, fair churches in several islands; but most remarkable is that of the Padri Olivetani, in S. Helen's island, for the rare paintings and carvings, with inlaid work, etc.

103

" Three days after, I passed over to Murano, famous for the best glasses in the world, where having viewed their furnaces, and seen their work, I made a collection of divers curiosities and glasses, which I sent for England by long sea. It is the white flints they have from Pavia, which they pound and sift exceedingly small, and mix with ashes made of a sea-weed brought out of Syria, and a white sand, that causes this manufacture to excel. The town is a Podestaria by itself, at some miles distant on the sea, from Venice, and like it built upon several small islands. In this place are excellent oysters, small and well-tasted like our Colchester, and they were the first, as I remember, that I ever could eat ; for I had naturally an aversion to them.

" At our return to Venice, we met several gondolas full of Venetian ladies, who come thus far in fine weather to take the air, with music and other refreshments. Besides that, Murano is itself a very nobly built town, and has divers noblemen's palaces in it, and handsome gardens.

" In coming back, we saw the islands of S. Christopher and S. Michael, the last of which has a church enriched and incrusted with marbles and other architectonic ornaments, which the monks very courteously shewed us. It was built and founded by Margaret Emiliana of Verona, a famous courtezan, who purchased a great estate, and by this foundation hoped to commute for her sins. We then rowed by the isles of S. Nicholas, whose church, with the monuments of the Justinian family, entertained us awhile : and then got home.

" The 31st October, being my birth-day, the nuns of S. Catherine's sent me flowers of silk-work. We were very studious all this winter till Christmas, when, on Twelfth-Day, we invited all the English and Scots in town to a feast, which sunk our excellent wine considerably.

"In January, Signor Molino was chosen Doge of Venice, but the extreme snow that fell, and the cold, hindered my going to see the solemnity, so as I stirred not from Padua till Shrovetide, when all the world repair to Venice to see the folly and madness of the Carnival; the women, men and persons of all conditions disguising themselves in antique dresses, with extravagant music and a thousand gambols, traversing the streets from house to house, all places being then accessible and free to enter. Abroad, they fling eggs filled with sweet water, but sometimes not over sweet. They also have a barbarous custom of hunting bulls about the streets and piazzas, which is very dangerous, the passages being generally narrow. The youth of the several wards and parishes contend in other masteries and pastimes, so that it is impossible to recount the universal madness of this place during this time of licence. The great banks are set up for those who will play at bassett; the comedians have liberty, and the operas are open; witty pasquils are thrown about, and the mountebanks have their stages at every corner. The diversion which chiefly took me up was three noble operas, where were excellent voices and music, the most celebrated of which was the famous Anna Rencia, whom we invited to a fish dinner after four days in Lent, when they had given over at the theatre. Accompanied with an eunuch whom she brought with her, she entertained us with rare music, both of them singing to a harpsichord. It growing late, a gentleman of Venice came for her, to shew her the galleys, now ready to sail for Candia. This entertainment produced a second, given us by the English consul of the merchants inviting us to his house, where he had the Genoese, the most celebrated bass in Italy, who was one of the late opera band. This diversion held us so late at night, that, conveying a gentlewoman who

P

had supped with us to her gondola at the usual place of landing, we were shot at by two carbines from another gondola, in which were a noble Venetian and his courtezan unwilling to be disturbed, which made us run in and fetch other weapons, not knowing what the matter was till we were informed of the danger we might incur by pursuing it farther.

" The next day I was conducted to the Ghetto, where the Jews dwell together as in a tribe or ward, where I was present at a marriage. The bride was clad in white, sitting in a lofty chair, and covered with a white veil ; then two old Rabbis joined them together, one of them holding a glass of wine in his hand, which, in the midst of the ceremony, pretending to deliver to the woman, he let fall, the breaking whereof was to signify the frailty of our nature, and that we must expect disasters and crosses amidst all enjoyments. This done, we had a fine banquet, and were brought into the bride-chamber, where the bed was dressed up with flowers, and the counterpane strewed in works. At this ceremony we saw divers very beautiful Portuguese Jewesses, with whom we had some conversation."

I have given so much of Evelyn's picture of Venice in the middle of the seventeenth century because it is little known, and is perhaps the fullest description of the city, as I have said, anywhere to be found. But he shews us the outward aspect of the city only. For a picture of the life of the place at this time we must go to other writers, for instance to Saint-Didier [1] and to Amelot de la Houssaye.[2] In these two precious and

[1] De Saint-Didier : *La Ville et la République de Venise* (1680).
[2] A. de la Houssaye : *Histoire du Gouvernement de Venise* (1676).

curious works we see with how extraordinary a carelessness Venice went on the road of death. There it is we have a picture of the degeneracy of the aristocracy, the most fatal symptom of all in an aristocratic State. The absence of any moral sense among the Venetian nobility, their cynical immorality, would almost seem to have been encouraged by the Government as the best means of obliterating thought and criticism and all hope of reform. The State became like a mighty building which has been left too long unrepaired and unrestored for its safety, but still presents an imposing appearance. Saint-Didier in speaking of the life of the youthful nobility tells us that they prided themselves on being libertines and gamblers. They by no means kept to one mistress, and their parents gave them the money necessary for their pleasures or at any rate shut their eyes to their disordered life. He records that the son of a considerable official became so amorous of one of the more beautiful courtesans that he actually took up his abode in her house. The afflicted father besought him to bring the lady to his home, since then he would at any rate see his son occasionally. Other writers endorse what Saint-Didier tells us, and assure us further that the mothers are the first to seek out courtesans for their sons in order to save them from contamination and disease. When these mothers have bargained with the mother and father of some poor girl, all their relations come to congratulate them as coolly as though a proper marriage contract had been signed.

Saint-Didier tells the following story :

" I found myself," he says, " one day by chance at a reception of this sort. It was already some time that a gentleman, a stranger to me, had been in treaty for a girl. Her aunt had brought her to his house, but as he hesitated to come to a definite decision, because as he thought

107

the girl was not plump enough and her breast was not well enough formed for him, the aunt told him that there could be no further delay, as the Father Confessor of one of the first convents in Venice, which she named, had begun to treat for the girl and had already made a reasonable offer."

Both Saint-Didier and Amelot de la Houssaye inform us that the young men of the Venetian nobility more often than not had a mistress in common, who instead of being a subject of discord between them was a bond of friendship !

Marriage, according to Amelot de la Houssaye, was generally considered a purely civil ceremony entered into for reasons of State or of family politics or for money reasons. As for these wives, they seem to have lived a life almost enclosed, if we are to believe the observers of the time. They live in retirement and privacy, we read ; they neither visit nor speak when they meet their equals, unless they happen to be great friends, which is rare in such a society. For the most part they remain at home, always *en déshabillé* excepting on festas and when they go to church, which is about all they do, at least those do whose husbands are not too jealous. There they find their distraction, and there they remain for hours, as long as they can indeed. Of the six or seven hundred noble ladies in Venice only about fifty or sixty are ordinarily to be seen in public, except on special occasions, when it is to be noted that their beauty is not very striking.

Amelot de la Houssaye definitely declares that the toleration and protection of courtesans by the State is the one evil out of which the Venetian Government has known how to draw good, delivering itself thus from the trouble of otherwise finding occupation for the young nobles, who having nothing at all to do would have occupied themselves with politics. This surely is the most cynical and suicidal policy that has ever been followed by a great State.

All this folly gathered itself together and expended itself in the Carnival when the whole city appeared in masques and fantastic dress, mothers carrying their infants in masques in their arms, and men and women even going thus to market. Of course the great rendezvous was the Piazza di S. Marco where all the city met till the place was so crowded that it was almost impossible to move. The Carnival was, it seems, the only occasion during the year when the married women of the nobility had an opportunity for intrigue. They were also used to go masked during these days which were in fact, or appear to have been in the memoirs of the time, a regular carnival of love-making. And when night fell and the Piazza began to empty the *ridotti* began, the gambling halls, into which all comers seem to have been invited, the young nobles taking the bank. The most famous of these *ridotti* at Carnival was that nearest to the Piazza where *bassetta* was played. It consisted of several rooms which were always so crowded that it was almost impossible to move from one to the other, though all were as silent as a church. There too you might see the married women sipping their sweet drinks, in a velvet *loup*.

## XI

## VENICE IN THE EIGHTEENTH CENTURY.

THE corruption of manners that had now been long characteristic of Venice in her decadence, perhaps reached its summit in the following century. Venice was now the resort of all the gilded youth of Europe, the great pleasure city of the West, and the number of distinguished men who have left us a picture of her gradually increases all through the eighteenth century till the fall of the Republic in 1796. Casanova, Rousseau, Gozzi, Goldoni, the Président de Brosses, and I know not how many others are full of Venice, and each in his own fashion has left us a picture which forbids any doubt as to the corruption of the Republic.

Nor was it only that manners were lax and licence in all matters of sexual morality outrageous. Every kind of ne'er-do-well, swindler, blackmailer and humbug abounded ; so long as their business was not political they were not interfered with. We know too that amid all this irreligion and atheism, superstition, that worst corruption of the intellect, abounded.

"THE RIVA"

It is indeed Casanova himself, perhaps the most characteristic son of Venice of the whole of the eighteenth century, who tells us in the very opening of his ever-living book, how, suffering as a child of eight from a continual bleeding of the nose, his grandmother Marzia, whose favourite he was, took him, very weak and ill from loss of blood, in a gondola to Murano to be treated by a witch.

"Having alighted from the gondola," he says, "we went into a hovel, where we found an old woman seated on a stump-bed, holding between her hands a black cat, and having five or six others about her. She was a sorceress. The two old women held a long discourse, of which it is probable that I was the subject. At the end of this dialogue in the dialect of Forll, the sorceress, having received from my grandmother a silver ducat, opened a chest, took me in her arms, put me inside and shut me in, telling me not to be afraid, which alone would have been enough to inspire me with fear if I had had any sense, but I was a blockhead. I remained quiet in a corner of the chest holding my handkerchief to my nose, for I still bled, and for the rest utterly indifferent to the hubbub that I heard without. I caught by turns the sound of laughing, crying, singing, screaming, and beating on the chest ; but it was all the same to me. At length I was taken out : the bleeding had stopped. . . . It would be ridiculous no doubt to attribute my healing to these extravagances, but I think one would be wrong to deny absolutely that they contributed to it. . . . Every day some phenomenon shows us our ignorance, and I think it is this which makes it so rare to find a *savant* entirely free from all superstition. No doubt such beings as sorcerers have never existed ; but it is not less true that their power has always existed for those to whom the cunning have had talent enough to make them believed in."

This ironical reflection reminds us of M. Bergeret's remarks to M. Goubin in Anatole France's inimitable ghost story *Putois*.

"—Cher maître, demanda M. Goubin, comment agit-il, puisqu'il n'existait pas ?

—Il avait une sorte d'existence, répondit M. Bergeret.

—Vous voulez dire une existence imaginaire, répliqua dédaigneusement M. Goubin.

—N'est-ce donc rien qu'une existence imaginaire ? s'écria le maître. Et les personnages mythiques ne sont-ils donc pas capables d'agir sur les hommes ? Réfléchissez sur la mythologie, monsieur Goubin, et vous vous apercevrez que ce sont, non point des êtres réels, mais des êtres imaginaires qui exercent sur les âmes l'action la plus profonde et la plus durable. . . ."

But with the amazing adventures of Casanova in Venice I will deal later. Let us now for a moment turn to the sentimental adventures of Rousseau, in this city of pleasure.

J. J. Rousseau, the author of the *Confessions*, sojourned for a year in Venice from August, 1743, to August, 1744, when he was thirty years old. He came there as secretary to the French ambassador, who he tells us was a complete imbecile, a mean fellow, and totally incapable of carrying out his functions. Rousseau describes himself as " irreproachable in a post very much in the public view, meriting and obtaining the *estime* of the Republic, of all the ambassadors with whom we were in correspondence and the affection of all the French in Venice." It is not, however, as an official that Jean Jacques interests us, but as a man of genius in Venice for the first time and for twelve months.

" I cannot take leave of Venice," he says, after a long account of his

112

official life there, " without saying something of the celebrated amusements of that city, or at least of the small part of them of which I partook during my residence there. I have shown how little in my youth I ran after the pleasures of youth, or those that have been so called, nor did my inclination change in Venice. The first and most pleasing of all my recreations was the society of men of merit. MM. le Blond, St. Cyr, Carrio, Altuna, and a gentleman of Forll, beside two or three Englishmen of great wit and information, and like the rest of my friends passionately fond of music, were among my acquaintances. All these gentlemen had their wives, female friends, or mistresses : the latter were most of them women of talent at whose apartments there were balls and concerts. There was but little play, for play is the resource of men when time hangs heavy on their hands.

" I had brought with me from Paris the prejudice of that city against Italian music ; but I had also by nature a sensibility and a niceness of taste which no prejudice could deceive. I soon contracted that passion for Italian music with which it inspires all capable of understanding it. In listening to *barcarolles* I found I had hitherto not known what singing was, and I now became so fond of the opera that, tired by talking, eating and playing in the boxes, I frequently withdrew from the company to another part of the theatre. There quite alone, shut up in my box I abandoned myself, notwithstanding the length of the performance, to the pleasure of enjoying it at ease to the end.

" One evening at the theatre of S. Chrysostom I fell into a sleep far deeper than I should have done had I been in bed. The loud and brilliant airs did not wake me. But how can I describe the delicious sensation given me by the soft harmonies of the angelic music, by which I was at length charmed out of my sleep ? What an awakening ! What ravishment ! What ecstasy ! when at the same time my eyes and my ears were opened. My first thought was that I was in Paradise. The ravishing air, which I still remember and shall never forget, began with these words :

> *" Conservami la bella*
> *Che si m'accende il cor . . . .*

" A kind of music far superior, in my view, to that of the Opera, and in Italy it has not its equal, nor even perhaps in the whole world, is that of the *Scuole*. The *Scuole* are houses of charity established for the education of young girls without fortune, to whom the Republic afterwards gives a portion, either in marriage or for the cloister. Every Sunday in the churches of each of the four *Scuole*, during vespers, motets with full choruses, accompanied by a great orchestra and composed and directed by the best masters in Italy, are sung in the galleries by girls only, not one of whom is more than twenty years of age. I cannot conceive of anything more voluptuous and moving than this music : the richness of the art, the exquisite taste of the vocal parts, the excellence of the voices, the justness of the execution—everything in these delightful concerts concurs to produce an impression which in my opinion no one can resist. Carrio and I never failed to be present at these vespers of the *mendicanti ;* and we were not alone ; the church was always full of the lovers of the art, and even the opera singers came there to form their taste on such excellent models. What annoyed me was the iron grate, which suffered nothing to escape but the sounds, and concealed from me the angels which were worthy of this music. I talked of nothing else. One day I spoke of it at Le Blond's. ' If you are so desirous,' said he, ' to see these little girls, it will be an easy matter to satisfy your wishes.

I am one of the administrators of the house, I will give you an opportunity of seeing them.' I did not let him rest until he had fulfilled his promise. In entering the *salon* which contained these beauties I so much longed to see, I felt a trembling of love which I had never before experienced. M. le Blond presented me to one after the other of these celebrated female singers, whose names and voices were all I knew of them. I saw Sophia, she was dreadful; Cattina, she had but one eye; Bettina, she was disfigured by the small-pox; scarce one of them was without some striking defect. Le Blond laughed at my surprise; however, two or three of them seemed to be tolerable, but these only sang in the choruses. I was in despair. During the refreshment we endeavoured to excite them and they soon responded. Ugliness does not exclude the graces, and I soon found that these they possessed. I said to myself: they cannot sing as they do without having intelligence and sensibility; in fact I soon saw them in a different light, and I left the house almost in love with each of those ugly faces. I had scarce courage to return to vespers: but I still found the singing delicious; and their voices so much embellished their faces that in spite of my eyes I always continued to think them beautiful."

Rousseau's adventures among the courtesans are perhaps scarcely worth repeating. One may content oneself with noting how he found to his surprise that Venice had invented the fascination of *lingerie*. " I found her," he says of one of his light o' loves, " I found her in *vestito di confidenza*, in an undress more than wanton, unknown to northern countries. I shall not amuse myself with describing it, though I recollect it perfectly. I will only say that it was edged with silk network ornamented with rose-coloured pompoms."

This is a delightful discovery, and perhaps was owing by the gods to the sentimentalist who can declare that he " entered the chambers of a woman of easy virtue as the sanctuary of love and beauty, and in her person I thought I saw the divinity." Well might one of them cry to him " *Lascia le donne, e studia la matematica.*"

They knew better than he who was to destroy this world, what in fact their business was. " As we conversed together," he tells us of one of these women, " I perceived a couple of pistols upon her toilette. ' Ah, ah,' said I, taking one of them up, ' this is a patch-box of a new construction : may I ask what is its use ? I know you have other arms which give more fire than these upon your table.' After a few more pleasantries of the same kind, she said to us, with an ingenuousness that rendered her still more charming, ' When I am complaisant to persons whom I do not love, I make them pay for the weariness they cause me ; nothing can be more just ; but if I suffer their caresses, I will not bear their insults, nor miss the first who shall be wanting in respect.' "

## XII

## CASANOVA AND VENICE.

LET us turn now to Casanova, another writer of Confessions, though in speaking of his inexhaustible book he says, " I shall not give to my story the name of Confessions, for since an extravagant man (Jean Jacques Rousseau) has so exalted the name of them I cannot possibly endure it ; but it shall be a Confession if ever there was one."

Jacques Casanova de Seingalt was born in Venice on April 2nd, 1725. His father had become an actor, and came to Venice in a troupe of comedians to play at the Teatro Grimani di San Samuele. Opposite the house where he lodged there lived a shoemaker named Girolamo Farusi, with his wife Marzia and their only daughter Zanetta, a beautiful girl aged sixteen. The young comedian fell in love with this girl and carried her off, for it was the only means of possessing her, for neither her father nor her mother would have consented to the match. The two young people having obtained the necessary documents and accompanied by two witnesses, presented themselves to the Patriarch of Venice, who gave them the nuptial benediction. That was in 1724 ; in the following year Jacques Casanova was born.

As I have said, the first thing Casanova could remember of his life was his grandmother taking him to the sorceress at Murano to be cured of a continual bleeding of the nose. This is curious, not only for the light it throws on Venetian customs, but because it was apparently for mixing himself up with necromancy that, at the request of the ecclesiastical inquisition, he was imprisoned in the Piombi till fifteen months later he made perhaps the most famous escape in history from the most infamous dungeons in the world. It remains uncertain, however, what really was the cause of his imprisonment.

He was taken by his grandmother to Padua to be educated. They went thither from Venice in a *burchiello* by the Brenta. This was the ordinary way of making the journey. Casanova describes the *burchiello* as a little floating house, with a long chamber in the midst and a small cabin at each end and a place for servants at the prow and the poop. The voyage took eight hours.

His studies finished, he returned to Venice and received minor orders, with the tonsure, at the hands of the Patriarch. The curé of S. Samuele accepted him and installed him in his church, and the Abbé de Grimani became his principal protector. But Casanova's life was too disordered even for the clergy of the day. He led a gay life, and let his hair, which he dressed most carefully in order to cut a good figure with the women, grow over the tonsure. This so annoyed the good curé that he crept into Casanova's chamber while he slept and cut his curls with a pair of scissors.

Casanova's career in the Church was short. It is amazing to think of him there at all, even in a minor capacity. It is even more amazing

118

to know that he actually preached a sermon in S. Samuele and apparently with success. It was his one and only achievement in this way, though not his only attempt. On a second occasion he was so drunk that he fell down in the pulpit to the enormous scandal even of that tolerant congregation.

" I was still at table with all the pleasant company (with the Comte de Mont-Réal and others) when a clerk came to tell me that they waited me in the sacristy. My stomach full and my head on fire I left and ran to the church and ascended into the pulpit. I said the exordium very well, and then I took breath; but scarcely had I pronounced the first words of the narration when I no longer knew what I was saying nor what I ought to say, and wishing to go on by force I beat the air, wandered, and blundered. What succeeded in disconcerting me was a confused murmur in all the auditorium which became restless, and where everyone easily perceived my discomfiture. I saw some of them leave the church, I thought I heard others laughing, I lost my head and all hope of getting myself out of the mess. It is impossible for me to say whether I made a show of falling in a swoon or whether in fact I fainted; all I know is that I let myself fall on the floor of the pulpit, striking my head against the wall. . . ." He fled to Padua, and this was the end of his career in the Church.

Up and down this wonderful book, indeed in almost every page of its earlier volumes, one sees the life of Venice at this time ebb and flow. Casanova himself might stand as a sort of symbol of the city. Here was a man among the most intelligent and remarkable of his time, full of an enormous energy and vitality, who spent his whole life, hours and days and weeks and months and years of labour in running after women, in seducing them and in being seduced, in satisfying them with his body and with his imagination : and at the end of his life there is nothing, nothing, a bitterness in the mind, a handful of dust and ashes. And yet perhaps that is too despondent a view; for, as to Venice there remains and will remain all her beauty of architecture and painting, so Casanova has left us his book, an ignoble but a fascinating record of how he lived and wasted his time, of his crimes and his follies and his foolish life illuminated by that amazing intellect which is as hard and as clear as crystal, throwing a light of irony over all his actions.

It was not only himself he understood : he understood Venice, and with his piercing and yet tolerant glance searches out the source of her corruption. Hear him on her conservatism.

In 1745 the Republic, he tells us, suppressed the galleasses. These great ships had been built from the most ancient times at great cost, and their utility, as he says, was null. A galleass had the body of a frigate and the oars of a galley and five hundred rowers to row it when there was no wind.

" Before good sense succeeded in suppressing these useless carcases there were great debates in the Senate. The great point of the opponents of the suppression was that it was necessary to respect and to conserve everything that was ancient. This malady is that of people who do not know how to identify themselves with the successive ameliorations which are the fruit of reason aided by experience : good people whom it is necessary to send to China or to the country of the Grand Lama, which would suit them much better than Europe. This point of view, ridiculous as it is, is one which has most force in Republics, because they must tremble at the word novelty in frivolous as in important things.

120

Superstition besides belongs to them. What the Republic of Venice will never reform is the galleys, first because she has need of these ships for sailing at all times in a narrow sea despite the lack of wind, and then because she would not know what to do with the men she has condemned to the galleys."

He comments again later on the aristocratic oligarchy of Venice. " In the beginning of 1750 I gained at the lottery a *terno* of three thousand ducats. Fortune made me this present at a moment when I had no need of it, for I had passed the autumn in holding the bank and I had won. It was in a casino where no noble Venetian dare present himself, because one of the associates was the ambassador of Spain. The nobles, too, upset the bourgeois ; and this always happens in an aristocratic government where equality cannot in fact exist except between members of the governing class."

The mind that could comprehend the causes of the phenomena he witnessed in so clear a fashion was for the most part engaged in quite other business and was always overwhelmed by the mere physical vitality of the man. No one enjoyed the famous Venetian Carnival more than he, or took a more boy-like pleasure in the rowdyism and practical jokes that were practised at that season.

" Often we would pass the nights in wandering through the different quarters of the town, inventing and carrying out every sort of impertinence imaginable. One of our favourite pleasures was to set adrift from the quays private gondolas and to let them go as they would with the current in the canals while we enjoyed in advance the curses that would be hurled at us in the morning. Often also we went to awaken in great haste eminent *sages femmes*, conjuring them to go to such-and-such a lady

R

who was not even *enceinte* and who treated them as mad when they arrived. We did the same with the doctors, whom we made run half dressed to the house of such-and-such a grand seigneur who was perfectly well. The priests had their turn ; we sent them to administer extreme unction to some husband who was sleeping peacefully with his wife and thinking of anything rather than of dying. We destroyed bell-ropes in all houses, and when we passed an open door we went in on tip-toe and frightened the sleepers by crying to them that the door of their house was open. One very dark night we upset a great table of marble, a sort of monument in the Piazza S. Angelo where at the time of the League of Cambray the commissioners paid the recruits of S. Mark, and which enjoyed a sort of veneration. We sounded the tocsin and stopped the clock and bilked the gondoliers till all the town was full of complaint. . . ."

It is, too, to Casanova that we owe a description of the night *caffè*.

" In each of the sixty-two parishes of the city of Venice there is a great cabaret that they call a *magazzino*. It is open all night, and the wine is sold more cheaply there than in other places. You can also eat there, but you have to have what you want brought in from the neighbouring pork butcher, who by privilege and for this business keeps his shop open all night. These establishments are very useful to the poor. One never sees there the nobles or the bourgeoisie or even an artisan in good circumstances. There you find little separate rooms, where on a table quite bare, surrounded by forms, an honest family or some friends can enjoy themselves in a decent manner."

But all the carnival life of the city passes before us in these pages. Casanova used to meet his mistress under the statue of Colleoni. " At two hours after sunset precisely I saw my mistress alight from the gondola masked as a woman. We went to the opera at the theatre of S. Samuele, and at the end of the grand ballet we went to the *ridotto* where she much amused herself in looking at the patrician ladies who alone have the privilege of sitting there with the face uncovered. After we had promenaded for half an hour we passed into the hall of the great bankers. She stopped before the table of Seigneur Mocenigo, who was the greatest of all the patrician players. Having nothing to do at the moment he was carelessly leaning towards the ear of a masked lady that I recognized; it was Mme. Marie Pitani, whose adorer he was.

"My mistress having asked me whether I wished to play, and I having answered no:

" ' I'll go halves with you,' she said.
And without waiting for a reply she drew out her purse and placed some gold on a card. The banker without disturbing himself shuffled, cut, and my mistress won and doubled her stake. The banker paid, then took another pack of cards and continued to talk to his neighbour, showing himself indifferent to the four hundred sequins which my beauty had already placed on the same card. The banker continued to talk; my mistress said to me in good French, ' Our game isn't big enough to interest Monsieur; let us go away.'

"She took away her card, and I collected the gold which I put in my pocket, without replying to Monsieur, who said to me, ' Your masque is really too intolerant.' I rejoined my beautiful gambler who was surrounded.

"Soon we stopped before the bank of Seigneur Pierre Marcello, a charming young man who had beside him Mme. Venier, sister of Seigneur M——. My mistress played; she lost five stakes in succession. Having

123

no more money she took the gold from my pocket in handfuls, and in four or five coups she broke the bank. She left, and the noble banker saluted her, complimenting her on her good luck. After having gathered up all the gold gained, I gave her my arm and we departed : but perceiving that many followed us out of curiosity I took a gondola from the *traghetto* that I directed to land us where I wished. It is thus at Venice that one escapes from too inquisitive looks. After supper I counted our gain and I found that my part amounted to a thousand sequins."

Perhaps I might add that Casanova's chief mistress at this time, the lady who won the sequins for him, was a beautiful nun. Sometimes she came to him masked as a man, more often as a woman, and they enjoyed themselves together all over Venice, and in his sumptuous apartments at Murano which had belonged to the English ambassador.

The life of the convents at that time in Venice was utterly corrupted. Casanova himself gives us the following picture of a ball in the convent parlour.

" Laure had informed me that on a certain day there was to be a ball in the great parlour of the convent, and I was determined to go there in mask, but disguised in such a fashion that my two mistresses would not be able to recognize me. I went masked *en Pierrot*, a disguise which hid me completely. I was sure that my two charming mistresses would be at the grill and that I should have the pleasure of seeing them and comparing them from near by.

" At Venice during the carnival this innocent pleasure is permitted in the convents. The public dances in the parlour, and the sisters from within, behind their ample grills, look on at the fête. At the end of the

124

"BOAT BUILDING"

day the ball finishes and everyone goes away and the poor recluses are for long happy with the pleasure their eyes have given them.

" I have said that the dress of Pierrot is of all disguises that which hides me best ; but in order that the dress should not interfere too much with one's movements, it is necessary to have nothing underneath it, and in winter so slight a covering has many disadvantages. I took no notice of these, but having taken some soup I got into a gondola and went off to Murano. I had not even a mantle, and in my pockets I only had my handkerchief, my purse, and the key of the casino.

" I entered, the parlour was full ; but owing to my costume everyone made way for me, for at Venice it is extremely rare to see a Pierrot. I advanced bearing myself like a simpleton according to the character demanded by my costume, and I entered the circle of dancers. After having considered the punches, the pantaloons, the harlequins, and the scaramouches I approached the grills, and I saw all the nuns and the *pensionnaires*, the former seated, the latter standing, and there were my two mistresses very intent on the fête. I approached a pretty harlequin and seized her by the hand to dance a minuet. Everyone laughed at me and made room for us. My harlequin danced beautifully, in character with the mask she wore and I too according to mine, so that I set all the company laughing. After the minuet I danced twelve *furlanes* with the greatest vigour. Out of breath, I let myself fall, pretending to sleep. I pretended to snore and everyone respected the sleep of Pierrot. Then a *contre dance* in which I took no part went on for an hour, but when it was finished suddenly a harlequin with the impertinence permitted to her costume began to beat me soundly with her sword. In my character of Pierrot having no arm I seized her round the waist and carried her,

125

still beating me, round the parlour at a run. I put her down then and having seized her weapon I chased her before me amid the shouts of laughter of the spectators and cries from the harlequin. . . ."

Such were the convents in Venice in the middle of the eighteenth century. Casanova is by no means alone in so describing them ; every writer of the time is full of their follies.

If Casanova only bears witness among a crowd of others to the general corruption of Venetian manners at this time, he is our only authority for a darker side of that failing oligarchical State. I mean the terrible life of the dungeons into which a man might be thrown for eight days or five years or for life without any sort of trial or even explanation, in fact without knowing why he was imprisoned at all. Casanova himself, who was condemned for five years, and who actually spent fifteen months in the *Piombi* before he made his marvellous escape, never knew to the end of his life the true cause of his apprehension, nor are we to-day by any means sure of it.

Casanova was arrested on the 26th July, 1755, by the Tribunal. Certain books of necromancy were found in his room, and he tells us that public opinion considered that he had been arrested by the Inquisition because he was in course of forming a new sect. Messer Grande took him away in a gondola to his offices, and later the order was given to take him again in gondola to the *Piombi*. "We entered a gondola and after a thousand detours by small canals we entered the Grand Canal, and arrived at the quay of the prison. After mounting many stairways we traversed an enclosed bridge (the Bridge of Sighs) which made the communication between the Ducal Palace and the Prison over the canal called Rio di Palazzo. On the other side of this bridge there is a gallery

126

which we traversed, and passing through a chamber we entered another, and I was presented to an individual dressed in the robe of a patrician who, after measuring me with his eye, said, ' Put him in *deposito*.'

" Messer Grande handed me over to the gaoler of the *Piombi*, who was there with an enormous bunch of keys, and who, followed by two constables, made me mount two little stairways, at the top of which we traversed a gallery, then a second, separated the one from the other by a locked door, then still another, at the bottom of which another door was opened which gave access to a filthy chamber, badly lighted by a window very high up. I took this place to be my prison, but I was in error, for taking an enormous key the gaoler opened a heavy iron door, three and a half feet high, having in the middle a round hole about eight inches in diameter, and ordered me to enter. I was at the moment examining a machine of iron solidly built into the masonry. This machine, I was informed, was for the purpose of strangling. It was very ingenious, and I asked my gaoler whether it was not he who turned the handle. He did not reply, and having made a sign to me to enter, to do which I had to bend nearly double, he locked me in, and immediately asked me through the grill of the door what I wanted to eat.

" ' I have not yet thought,' I answered. And he went away, locking all the doors with care.

" Dejected and stunned, I leant on my elbows on the sill of the grill. It was an opening two feet square, closed by six bars of iron, each an inch thick, leaving sixteen spaces of five inches. This opening would have left my cell clear enough if a square beam, one of the chief supports of the roof, eighteen inches wide, had not entered the wall over the window that was obliquely opposite. The beam intercepted the light that entered

127

the terrible outer chamber. After making the round of the miserable cell, with my head bowed, for it was only five and a half feet high, I found, feeling my way as I went, that it formed three parts of a square of from six to seven feet each way. The fourth side consisted of an alcove for a bed ; but I found no bed, no table, nor chair, nor furniture of any kind, except a tub or trough whose use one may divine and a plank fixed to the wall, a foot wide and four feet from the floor. Upon this I threw my silk mantle, my fine coat and my hat bordered with *point d'espagne* and adorned with a beautiful white feather. The heat was extreme and mechanically I went instinctively towards the little grill, the only place where I could rest myself on my elbows. I could not see the window, but I saw the light which illumined the outer chamber and certain rats of a frightful grossness who moved about, altogether at their ease ; for these terrible animals, the very sight of which I abhor, came right up under my grill without showing the least fear. At this disagreeable view I hastened to shut with the shutter the round hole in the middle of the door, for their coming there froze my blood. I fell into a profound reverie my arms all the time crossed on the high sill, and so I passed eight hours in the silence and without making a movement.

" At the sound of the clock, which struck twenty-one o'clock, I began to rouse, and I experienced some inquietude at not seeing anyone who might bring me something to eat, and the things I had need of to enable me to sit down. It seemed to me that at least they should have brought me a chair and some bread and water. I had no appetite, but they did not know that ; and never in my life have I had a mouth so parched and so bitter. I thought, however, it was certain that before the end of the day someone would appear ; but when I heard twenty-four o'clock

128

strike I became furious, beating the door and kicking it, cursing and accompanying with shouts and cries all the vain noise that my strange situation excited me to make. After more than an hour of this furious exercise, seeing no one, and not having the least idea whether or no anyone had heard my cries, enveloped in darkness, I closed the grill for fear the rats should creep into my cell and I threw myself at full length on the floor. To be thus utterly abandoned did not seem to me human, and I made up my mind that the barbarous inquisitors had decided on my death. Thinking what I could have done to merit such treatment did not take me long, for the most scrupulous investigation of my action did not discover anything that convinced me. I was a libertine, a gambler and I spoke my mind, also I was in the habit of only thinking of how to enjoy life; but in all that I could not see any crime against the State. Nevertheless, seeing myself treated as a criminal, I was filled with rage and despair against the horrible despotism which oppressed me, and I expressed myself in terms which shame forces me to allow my readers to divine and that I shall not repeat here. However, excitement and hunger began to make themselves felt. These, however, and the thirst which devoured me, and the hardness of the floor on which I lay could not prevent exhausted nature from claiming her rights, and I slept.

" My robust constitution had need of sleep, and in a young person in good health this imperious need silences all others, and it is in this sense above all that one may call sleep the benefactor of men.

" The strokes of midnight awakened me. How frightful is awakening when it makes us regret the illusions of oblivion. I could not realize that I had spent three hours without experiencing any pain. Lying on my left side, without moving, I stretched out my right arm to get my handkerchief that I remembered to have put there. I felt about. God, what was my surprise when my hand seized another cold as ice. Fright shot through me from head to foot, and my hair stood on end on my head. Never in my life have I been seized with such terror, and I never believed myself capable of it. I passed three or four minutes in a sort of faint, not only without moving but without being able to think. When I once more came to myself I tried to think that the hand I had seized was only an effect of my imagination, and in this hope I again stretched out my arm, and again I found the same hand. Numb and trembling with horror I gave a piercing scream, and pushing away the hand I held I drew back my arm shivering. Soon when I was a little calmer and capable of reflection I decided that while I had slept they had brought in and deposited near me a corpse ; I was sure that when I lay down it was not there. It is the corpse, I thought, of some wretch they have strangled and they wish to warn me of what is reserved for me. This thought exasperated me, I became furious, and all my fright gave way to rage. A third time I stretched out my arm towards the icy hand, I seized it to assure myself of the atrocious truth, and wishing to get up, I leaned on my left elbow, and then I knew that it was my other hand that I held ; dead under the weight of my body and with the hardness of the floor, it had lost its heat, movement and feeling.

"This adventure, in spite of its comic side, did not cheer me ; it gave me instead many black thoughts. I perceived that I was in a place where, if the false appeared true, the true might also appear false, where the understanding lost half its privileges and where the imagination victimized the reason with chimerical hope or frightful despair."

It was in this frightful cell which was in darkness for nineteen out of the twenty-four hours, fearfully hot in summer and freezing cold in winter, infested with vermin and, as we have seen, about which rats prowled, that Casanova was to spend the next year of his life.

But what were these prisons ?

" The *Piombi*," says Casanova, " the prisons destined to hold State criminals, were nothing else than the garrets of the Ducal Palace, and it is from the great plaques of lead with which this palace is covered that they get their name. They can only be reached by the gates of the palace or from the prisons, or by the bridge of which I have already spoken, and that is called the Bridge of Sighs. . . . Beside the *Piombi* there are the nineteen other frightful prisons underground in the same Ducal Palace, terrible hiding-places destined for the wretches whom one does not wish to condemn to death, though their crimes make them worthy of it. . . . These subterranean prisons resemble tombs, and are called *Pozzi*, because they always have two feet of water in them, which penetrates there from the sea by the same grill from which they receive what light they have. The grill is only a foot square. One wretch who died in the *Pozzi* while I was in the *Piombi* had passed thirty-seven years of his life there."

These *Pozzi* were, as Casanova says, only used for the worst criminals, or for traitors to the State. The *Piombi* came next in terror, but as his gaoler Laurent tells him, those imprisoned there " were all persons of the greatest distinction and criminals, the reason for whose arrest it was impossible for the most curious of men to discover."

Casanova spent altogether fifteen months in prison before he effected his escape. The story of his imprisonment is one of the most fascinating ever written, and very much enhances our respect for the man who was able to carry it through. The enormous ability of the author of the *Mémoires* is not so surprising as his good sense. Thus when he had been in prison some time he asked for books. Those he demanded were denied him, but the Inquisition sent him others, namely *La Cité Mystique* by Sœur Marie d'Agrada, and the work of a Jesuit, Caravita on the Adoration of the Sacred Heart of Jesus.

Of the latter he remarks : " Of all the human parts of our Divine Mediator it is this (the Heart) which according to this author we ought especially to adore ; a singular idea, only possible to an ignorant madman. The reading of this book revolted me from the first page, for the heart does not appear to me more worthy of respect than the lung or indeed any other part." It might be Huysmans speaking.

The book of Marie d'Agrada interested him a little. It had been printed by permission of " the very holy and very horrible inquisition." Very far, however, from exciting in Casanova a spirit of fervour, a simple zeal for religion, it excited him to consider fabulous all religion, both mystical and dogmatic. " I began to feel myself obsessed. I soon perceived the disease that the Sœur d'Agrada communicated to my spirit already enfeebled by melancholy and bad nourishment, the bad air and the horrible uncertainty they kept me in regarding my fate." He flung away these works of the decadence and they gave him Boëthius.

His escape was begun in the following manner. Having found in the outer chamber a bolt, he fashioned it into a sort of dagger. With this he cut away the floor under his bed. After weeks of work and sweat and fear, when he had cut through not only the planks but a floor of mosaic beneath them and could, through a small hole, already see into the room below and had determined to escape the next day, the gaoler came to him and

"PONTE DEL PARADISO"

cheerily informed him he was that very morning to be moved to a better and more healthy cell!

He had to go, there was no choice, and of course all his work was discovered. The gaoler, however, fearing for his own skin, did not inform the authorities of Casanova's attempt. In his new quarters, which overlooked the Schiavone, he still had his dagger, but could not use it as he was suspect. However, he contrived to pass it to a fellow-prisoner in the binding of a folio Bible. This man under his direction cut a hole in the wall and covered it up with the picture of a saint. Everything worked successfully, and though nearly ruined at the last moment, he and his companion stood free in the Piazza di S. Marco at midnight on October 31st. It had been prophesied to him by a Jesuit father that he would be free on the day of his saint. November 1st was All Saints. He got away from Venice to terra firma and went to Paris.

But these prisons of which Casanova has so much to say must have been far more terrible places even than they appear to-day, and the secrecy and tyranny of the Republic were among the nightmares of Italy. At the same time, as the Président de Brosses remarks, " It is not necessary to believe all the evil that is said of the Venetian Government, but only the greater part."

The Président gives much the same account of Venetian manners as we find in Rousseau and Casanova. " There is no place in the world where liberty and licence reign more absolutely than they do in Venice. If one does not mix oneself up with politics one can do anything else one likes. Nothing here that is natural shocks anyone. For everything that a sane morality would call evil there is complete impunity. Yet the blood is so sweet here that in spite of the opportunity that the universal

133

masquerade gives, and the chances of the night, the streets and above all the unprotected bridges whence one may easily push a man without being perceived, there do not occur more than four such accidents in a year, and these only among strangers. You can thus gauge whether the stories of Venetian daggers are well founded."

He goes on to tell us that when a woman marries she becomes a piece of furniture in her husband's house, and that the only chance you have of seeing her unattended is in a gondola.

What he has to tell us of the convents quite bears out Casanova, though he adds that in his day " the profits of the nuns who were yesterday in full possession of this life of gallantry have much diminished." Still, he tells us, there are even yet a good number who still enter upon this life with distinction and even emulation. Even at the time of his visit there was a furious competition going on between three convents of the city as to which of them should supply a mistress for the new Papal Nuncio. All the nuns he has seen in various convents behind the grills, he says, talk all the time Mass is going on and laugh together. They seemed to him pretty and excellently dressed to set off their beauty. They wore a very pretty coif, a simple habit, but well cut, almost always of white, which leaves the shoulders and the breast bare.

As for the courtesans, they are a really respectable body. " It is not necessary to believe, as is said, that the number is so great that you walk on them ; that is only at Carnival time, when you find as many under the arcades of the Piazza as you do women abed elsewhere. Altogether there are not in Venice more than twice as many as there are in Paris ; but they are very busy and very much sought after."

Altogether the memoirs of the time seem to shew us a corruption so general and so shameless that our sorrow at the tragedy which befell the city at the end of the century is very much mitigated.

It is not quite so violent a picture of Venice that we get in the Letters of Lady Mary Wortley Montagu ; but that is natural, and the picture she paints is quite as frivolous as any. She tells us, though, that the customs were changing, and that Venice would hardly be known for the same country as it had been twenty years before. Living was still very cheap, and the whole town given up to the Carnival. Writing to her husband in June, 1740, she devotes a page to the description of a regatta on the Grand Canal, the subject of one of Canaletto's most charming pictures.

" You seem to mention the regatta in a manner as if you would be pleased with a description of it. It is a race of boats : they are accompanied by vessels which they call Piotes, and Bichones, that are built at the expense of the nobles and strangers that have a mind to display their magnificence ; they are a sort of machines adorned with all that sculpture and gilding can do to make a shining appearance. Several of them cost one thousand pounds sterling, and I believe none less than five hundred ; they are rowed by gondoliers dressed in rich habits, suitable to what they represent. There was enough of them to look like a little fleet, and I own I never saw a finer sight. It would be too long to describe every one in particular ; I shall only name the principal : the Signora Pisani Mocenigo's represented the Chariot of the Night, drawn by four sea horses, and showing the rising of the moon accompanied with stars, the statues on each side representing the hours to the number of twenty-four, rowed by gondoliers, in rich liveries, which were changed three times, all of equal richness, and the decorations changed also to the dawn of Aurora, and the midday sun, the statues being new dressed every time, the first in

135

green, the second time red, and the last blue, all equally laced with silver, there being three races. Signor Soranzo represented the Kingdom of Poland, with all the provinces and rivers in that dominion, with a concert of the best instrumental music in rich Polish habits; the painting and gilding were exquisite in their kinds. Signor Contarini's piote showed the Liberal Arts; Apollo was seated on the stern upon Mount Parnassus, Pegasus behind, and the Muses seated round him: opposite was a figure representing Painting, with Fame blowing her trumpet, and on each side Sculpture and Music in their proper dresses. The Procurator Foscarini's was the Chariot of Flora guided by Cupids and adorned with all sorts of flowers, rose-trees, etc. Signor Julio Contarini's represented the Triumphs of Valour; Victory was on the stern, and all the ornaments warlike trophies of every kind. Signor Correri's was the Adriatic Sea, receiving into her arms the Hope of Saxony. Signor Alvisio Mocenigo's was the Garden of the Hesperides; the whole fable was represented by different statues. Signor Querini had the Chariot of Venus drawn by doves, so well done they seemed ready to fly upon the water; the Loves and Graces attended her . . ." and so forth. This is the more decorative side of the manners Casanova and Rousseau and the Président de Brosses describe. They are at best an empty pageant, passing an open grave.

We perceive something of this eternal masquerade in the delightful pictures of Longhi and Carriera. They painted the life they saw around them as did those rude artizans who were responsible for the *buffo* pictures in which was depicted the life of the common people, their fêtes and holidays.

At the same time we cannot forget that there was another side to all this: that the sober and careful pencil, careful for beauty, of Canaletto,

136

was then busy making Venice immortal and that Guardi was watching the wind on the lagoon and Tiepolo was looking up into the sky to descry our Lady enthroned, and seraphs on the wing.

The Venice in which such men as these worked, which such men could delight in, cannot have been as worthless as the memoir writers of the times have led us to believe. And yet it is not in the works of a painter concerned with the outward appearance, seeking for beauty as others for money, that we can discern the truth. Venice was then no doubt far lovelier than she is to-day. If she was more corrupt, it is because she was still alive, still the capital of a Sovereign State, and still possessed at any rate of enough energy to go to the devil, while in silks and satins and perukes the Venetians, whose fathers had stormed Constantinople, smiled at Goldoni's comedies or chattered through a Mass by Lotti, or languidly sat out a concert in which the old-fashioned music of Monteverde mingled with a Toccata of Baldassare Galuppi.

T

## XIII

## VENICE IN THE NINETEENTH CENTURY.

IT was in 1796 that Venice fell, and as was just and right, for the Venetian policy was nothing if not aristocratic, before the great Soldier of the Revolution, in the mighty wind that swept all Europe. Eustace, in one of the best and most charming books that have ever been written on Italy, a book written within six years of that event, thus sums it up at the beginning of the nineteenth century.

" From a people so degraded, so lost to bold and manly sentiments, no generous exertions, no daring enterprise is to be expected in the hour of danger. It is their policy to temporize, to weigh chances, to flatter the great, contending Powers, and it must be their fate to sink under the weight of the victorious. Such was the destiny of Venice. After having first insulted, and then courted the French Republic, it at length, without the means of defence in its hands, resigned itself to hollow friendship, and sent a thousand boats to transport the armies of France from the mainland over the Lagoon into the very heart of the city. The English commodore in the Adriatic protested against such madness, and offered

138

to cover the city with his own ships, in vain ! The people, who are always the last to lose a sense of national honour, expressed their readiness to stand forth and to defend their country—in vain ! The nobles trembled for their Italian estates, and in the empty hope of saving their income they betrayed their country and submitted to plunder, to slavery and to indelible disgrace. Not one arm was raised, not one sword was drawn, and Venice fell, self-betrayed and unpitied. Her enemies punished her pusillanimity by pillaging her public and her private treasures, by defacing her edifices, by stripping her arsenal, by carrying away her trophies ; and then they handed her over as a contemptible prize to a foreign despot. A tremendous lesson to rich and effeminate nations to rouse them to exertion, and to prove, if such proof were wanting, that independence must be preserved, as it can only be obtained, by the sword ; that money may purchase arms, but not freedom ; that submission excites contempt ; and that determined heroic resistance, even should it fail, challenges and obtains consideration and honour."

The population of Venice previous to the entry of the French was reckoned at a hundred and fifty thousand souls ; and it was supposed at the time that it considerably decreased after that event. Eustace prophesies that it will diminish : " Deserted like Siena and Pisa, this city shall become a superb solitude, whose lonely grandeur will remind the traveller that Venice was once great and independent." But Eustace could not foresee the greatest political event of the nineteenth century in Europe—the establishment of the Italian kingdom.

The state of society in Venice in the first years of the nineteenth century was not so disastrous as the political fortunes of the city might lead us to suppose. The *casinos* were still places of resort, card parties and suppers. Various houses were open to strangers, and as Eustace found, balls and concerts and club dinners were frequently given, to all of which introduction was not difficult.

The Carnival was still distinguished by plays in the daytime and by masked balls at night; the theatres were at such times charmingly and even splendidly illuminated. Open all day and night, the theatres were the resort of the idle part of the community, who if they pleased passed all the twenty-four hours in the playhouse, fell asleep and awoke, went out and came in, still to find the play going on with its usual spirit.

But it is Byron who speaks for the first time in the new century the truth about Venice. " I have been familiar with ruins too long to dislike isolation," he writes to Moore, in a letter telling him of his intention to spend the winter in Venice, in November, 1816. But even he did not discern what Venice was to become. He spent more than two years there and it was there, and how rightly, that he became the accepted lover of Countess Guiccioli.

The innate virility of Byron, however, at the very beginning of his stay asserted itself. " By way of divertisement I am studying daily at an Armenian monastery the Armenian language. I found that my mind wanted something craggy to break upon ; and this—as the most difficult thing I could discover here for an amusement—I have chosen to torture me into attention." Perhaps that is the most cruel criticism Venice has ever had to bear.

Yet Byron could give you a picture of the place, which he refused to describe to Moore, as it was so like all the descriptions ever written. It pleased him as much as he expected, and he expected much. It was, he

140

"S. FRANCESCO DE DESERTO"

says, one of those places which one knows before one sees them. " I like the gloomy gaiety of their gondolas and the silence of their canals. I do not even dislike the evident decay of the city, though I regret the singularity of its vanished costume ; however, there is much left still ; the Carnival, too, is coming." And again : " S. Mark's and indeed Venice is most alive at night."

Yes, we begin to see the city we have loved, not as we love a real thing, but as we love something in a dream.

But the old state of things continued. " The general state of morals here is much the same as in the Doge's time ; a woman is virtuous (according to code) who limits herself to her husband and one lover ; those who have two, three or more are a little *wild ;* but it is only those who are indiscriminatingly diffuse and form a low connexion who are considered as overstepping the modesty of marriage. In Venice the nobility have a trick of marrying dancers and singers, and truth to say the women of their own order are by no means handsome ; but the general run, the women of the second and other orders, the wives of the merchants and pro-prietors and untitled gentry are mostly *bel sangue*, and it is with these that the more amatory connexions are usually formed. There are also instances of stupendous constancy. I know a woman of fifty who never had but one lover, who dying early, she became devout, renouncing all but her husband. She piques herself, as may be presumed, upon this miraculous fidelity, talking occasionally of it with a species of misplaced morality which is rather amusing. There is no convincing a woman here that she is in the smallest degree deviating from the rule of right or fitness of things in having one amoroso." Well, Byron was not the man to convince her.

While Byron went to the opera, or made love, or wrote delightful verses " with a black-eyed Venetian girl before me, reading Boccaccio," Shelley came to Venice and in his strangely clairvoyant way seems to have got at the truth.

" Venice which was once a tyrant (he had just seen the *Piombi* and the *Pozzi*) is now the next worse thing, a slave ; for in fact it ceased to be free or worth one regret as a nation, from the moment that the oligarchy usurped the rights of the people. Yet I do not imagine that it was ever so degraded as it has been since the French, and especially the Austrian, yoke. The Austrians take sixty per cent in taxes and impose free quarters on the inhabitants. A horde of German soldiers, as vicious and more disgusting than the Venetians themselves, insult these miserable people. I had no conception of the excess to which avarice, cowardice, superstition, ignorance, passionless lust, and all the inexpressible brutalities which degrade human nature, could be carried, until I passed a few days at Venice."

But the Venice of Byron and Shelley has passed away as completely as that of Rousseau and Casanova. It is not so we think of Venice to-day : but as a dream city, a place really outside reality, a refuge and a delight ; not in the past, but outside the world, or at any rate our experience of it. And as with so much else, it is Charles Dickens who first expresses this feeling and gives it force and utterance. He shews us Venice as just that, and describes it to us very perfectly as a vision coming to him in the old Market Place of Verona.

It is a ghostly city he sees, full of the night at first and hung with votive lamps before innumerable shrines, and the only sound is the sound of water. Then the dawn breaks over the domes of S. Mark's,

142

and lights up the streets of water and reveals the delicate, ineffable sky ; and the floating city unveils herself, and churches, towers, palaces, and prisons rise out of the still water which sucks softly at their walls and wells up into the secret places of the city and creeps along to the sea : "Noiseless and watchful, coiled round and round it in many folds like an old serpent : waiting for the time when people should look down into its depths for any stone of the old city that had claimed to be its mistress."

There, and for the first time, we have the authentic voice of the modern world speaking of Venice. All D'Annunzio's eloquence is but a descant upon this melody of Dickens.

It is this Venice, something not in the past, but outside the world, the city of a vision or a dream, that Turner paints with its vast conflagrations of sunset, its unimaginably tender and luminous dawns ; now veiling itself in a delicate and fragile mist of silver, now shining in the splendour and glory and gold of the sun ; a city no man shall ever see but in his own heart.

And for us at least this visionary city exists and will always exist, not only because Dickens and Turner and other great creative artists have shewn it to us. For us this dream city is really inhabited by dream people ; and how much more real they are than the most famous citizens of Venice ! For, when we hear the name of Venice, or look at a picture or drawing of her, it is not of Dandolo, or Faliero, or Aretino, or Titian, or Casanova we think, but of Desdemona and Othello, of Iago, and of Shylock and Portia and Jessica and Launcelot Gobbo. These people we know ; they are our friends, and they inhabit and express that dream city whose streets are waterways, whose houses and palaces and churches rise out of the sea.

143

Well, into this dream there crept in the year 1847 a shadow of reality. Venice, as we have seen, had become an appendage of the Empire in 1797 ; but when all Lombardy was seething with Italian nationalism, Venice too woke from sleep. The revolt was headed by a Venetian Jew, Daniele Manin, who with his friend Tommaseo, was arrested and thrown into prison by the Austrian Government. When the news of the revolution at Vienna reached Venice in the spring of 1848, the people rose *en masse* and demanded the liberation of their leaders. The Government yielded and even permitted the Venetians to form a civic guard to maintain order in the city. This guard quickly grew to be two thousand strong, the arsenal was seized, the Italians in the Austrian garrison deserted to the revolutionaries, and Austria was obliged to evacuate the city, and indeed most of the cities of Venetia. On March 24th the Venetians proclaimed the restoration of the Republic and Manin was elected, not Doge, but President.

But the Republic of S. Mark was as much a dream as we might suppose. It was without any reality or meaning. The real movement for Italian independence and nationality is far from Venice and further still from such a dream as this. The restless ghost of the Republic only brought back the Austrian. Suspected by Piedmont, without support and without hope, Venice was besieged. The eloquence and sentimentality of Manin inspired the Venetians to a long and hopeless and heroic resistance. Appeal after appeal was made to the Powers of Europe : none would intervene. Venice was blockaded by land and sea ; and when the fortress of Maghera fell the Austrian artillery was within range of the city. Venice capitulated on August 24th, 1849. The siege had lasted fifteen months. It was not as a Republic that Venice was to survive, but as one of the fairest jewels in the Crown of United Italy, into which she was incorporated after the war of 1866.

Venice as a city of the Italian kingdom resumed, and will probably more and more resume something of her great maritime importance. But it is not as one of the chief ports of the Adriatic that we think of her to-day, but still as that dream city, established not so much in the past, as outside the world. It is this fantastic and visionary city we see in the pictures of Mr. Brangwyn: a city overwhelmed by the sun or caught in the darkness of night, full of the violence of bright colours, vast shadows, enormous reflections, a fury of movement and of pleasure, and continual energy and enjoyment.

It is this Venice, too, that D'Annunzio gives us in *Fuoco*. " If its whole population were to emigrate, forsaking its houses, attracted by other shores, as once its own heroic youth were tempted by the arch of the Bosphorus in the time of the Doge Pietro Ziani, and no prayer were again to strike the sonorous gold of the curved mosaics, no oar were again to perpetuate with its rhythm the meditation of the silent stones, Venice would yet and for ever remain a City of Life. The ideal creatures guarded by its silence live in the whole past and in the whole future. We constantly find in them new concordances with the edifice of the Universe that is to be. . . ."

A city of life. . . . Yes, it is that after all which Venice has always been and will always be. It is so she appears to us, not less in her furious pleasures and carnivals, than in the enormous energy of her conquest and the long persistence of her domination. However variously, it is life which she expresses in expressing herself, sometimes with an amazing frivolity that is an astonishment to history ; sometimes with the same serious and concentrated effort that once made her the mistress of the sea. To us she must always remain an inspiration and a desire : in her beauty, her grace and her glory. I see her now as I saw her in the thunder of the terrible disaster that has destroyed our world, the most beautiful of all our cities, facing and outfacing, with an immortal and perfect courage, the violation of the Barbarian. In the darkness of those wonderful nights, in the cold glittering light of those terrible dawns, the deserted canals seemed fuller than ever of ancient poetry and all the ardour of the silent past. The stars would die in a sky almost green and rimmed with gold. Some mystery of light coming from the sea poured over the city, thrusting back the darkness like an enemy, and the churches and towers and palaces seemed miraculous, unsubstantial, aerial ; symbols of our achievement and mysteriously inviolate.

And as the cold faint wind blew from the sea, and my boat flew towards the dawn, past the ivory of the Ducal Palace, past San Giorgio flushed and tall, gradually the expanse of sea, and the strength of the sea wind, dominated everything ; and the city faded away as a dream.

146

# A Book of Bridges.

Pictures by FRANK BRANGWYN, R.A.   Text by W. SHAW SPARROW. Containing 36 Colour Plates, and 36 Line Drawings.   Crown 4to. 31s. 6d. net.

Also Large Paper Edition, limited to 75 numbered copies, for sale in England and America.   Crown folio (15×10).   Printed on hand-made paper, with an original lithograph by FRANK BRANGWYN, of which only the copies required for this Edition will be printed, after which it will be taken off the stone.   £5 5s.   (*Out of print.*)

"This beautiful and delightful book.  It is 'belles-lettres,' it is Art, and history and architecture all in equal parts . . . intensely interesting for the general reader as well as for the historian."
*Outlook.*

"The subject permits of a study of Brangwyn at his best, and the production of the plates in the book is consistent with the quality of the originals, so that the book itself is thoroughly artistic both in matter and in manner."—*Country Gentleman.*

"Mr. Sparrow's knowledge of Bridges is extensive and peculiar.  He is always telling us something that will be news, even to the 'pontist' of experience and prescience."—*Morning Post.*

"The 'Book of Bridges' is alive.   Its author is no Dryasdust to retail musty records.   From cover to cover we may search in vain for 'claycold' page or 'glacial' footnote, but all is in consent with the freedom of the beautiful pictures that represent the part of Mr. Brangwyn in a perfect collaboration.   By the combined art of these devout pontists we are brought to look at 'Bridges' with inquisitive eyes."—*Saturday Review.*

"It is gratifying to find that an artist like Mr. Frank Brangwyn and a *littérateur* like Mr. Shaw Sparrow, both ardent pontists, have collaborated to produce for our enjoyment the sumptuous 'Book of Bridges.'"—*Architect.*

# Prints & Drawings by Frank Brangwyn.

## With some other phases of his art.

By WALTER SHAW SPARROW.   Profusely Illustrated in colour, and black and white, with reproductions of drawings and pictures by FRANK BRANGWYN, R.A.   Demy 4to.   £2 12s. 6d. net.

Also special edition, limited to 60 numbered copies, printed on hand-made paper, containing a special lithograph and a special etching. (*Out of Print.*)

The reproductions from Mr. Brangwyn's prints, drawings and book illustrations, include four double pages in coloured collotype, sixteen illustrations in three, four and five colours, including a double page, and twenty-two illustrations in two colours, a double-page illustration cut in wood by the artist himself, and eight Rembrandt Photogravures of etchings.   There are also ninety black and white illustrations in the text.

"This handsome volume contains some of his finest creations. . . . The volume, which is excellently produced, the printing of the plates and letterpress being a joy to the connoisseur's eye, should find a place on the bookshelves of all lovers of British art."—*Morning Post.*

JOHN LANE THE BODLEY HEAD LIMITED, VIGO ST., W.1.